GARET ATWOOD ENVY SANDRA BERNHARD WIT SIMO
N LANGUAGE TORY BURCH PAT___ ___DY SMITH G
HOPRA EPIPHANIES CINDY CR___ ___TION
RA DERN MANNERS KEVIN DURAN___ ___AN F
CONFIDENCE JONATHAN FRANZEN ___ ROZ
AIS PATIENCE ELIZABETH GILBERT EPIPHANIES KIM
DID DESIGN MICHAEL MUSTO GOSSIP GOLDIE HAWN
INDY KALING INNOVATION DANNY MEYER STRATEGY
SELL ADVICE JEFF KOONS HABIT HODA KOTB FEAR K
O POSSESSION PETER MARINO DESIGN JOHN LITHG
OVE GEORGE R. R. MARTIN POWER LEIGHTON MEEST
NCE MIRA NAIR ENVY YOTAM OTTOLENGHI DISCIPLI
OKO ONO PATIENCE OZZY OSBOURNE FEAR CAMILLE
ABIT QUESTLOVE INTUITION ERIC RIPERT TIMING RZ
EDARIS WILLPOWER MARIA SHARAPOVA HABIT BART
ECTION CHERYL STRAYED ADVICE ELAINE STRITCH
LIMITS ALEX TREBEK MEMORY NEIL DEGRASSE TYSO
VIBES KENDALL JENNER YOUTH MICHAEL KORS HA
ILSON PROGRESS HANS ZIMMER LIMITS ANNE PASTE
BOARDMAN DISCIPLINE SUSAN LUCCI SECRETS NASS
GE SAUNDERS PROCRASTINATION GAVIN BROWN CO
A GOLDEN MEMORY WYLIE DUFRESNE THE FUTURE
NAOMI CAMPBELL CONFIDENCE JUDITH LEIBER LA
RAH JESSICA PARKER TRANSFORMATION JOHN RIDL
SCHAAL LUCK DAVID MILCH LUCK TOM DIXON DESI
LE STRATEGY JEFFREY EUGENIDES VULNERABILITY
PETITIVENESS LOIS LOWRY OPTIMISM RONI HORN

ON POINT

———

ON POINT

LIFE LESSONS FROM THE
"COLUMNISTS" INTERVIEWS OF WSJ. MAGAZINE

BLACK DOG
& LEVENTHAL
PUBLISHERS
NEW YORK

INTRODUCTION

WSJ. Magazine's Columnists feature, in which six people from different backgrounds and cultural pursuits—artists, scientists, fashion designers, CEOs, comedians, chefs and athletes, among others—weigh in on a single topic, has kicked off every issue since I became editor in chief in 2013. One part cocktail party chatter, one part philosophical debate, the page has, over its five years of existence, served as a monthly snapshot of the intellectual and emotional climate of the times.

It's also become, in a serendipitous way, a compendium of everyday wisdom. That's because the subjects covered by the column—love, power, fear, intuition, luck, envy, memory, confidence and so much more—have a broad appeal. The life lessons bubbling up from these short manifestos are as important to our readers as the headlines of the day. (And, speaking of news, in a nod to The Wall Street Journal, which WSJ. Magazine is wrapped and distributed inside every month, each columnist's portrait is rendered in the Journal's classic, hand-illustrated stipple style, referred to as a "hedcut" by the newsroom.)

The volume you hold in your hands is the first time this pithy opinion page and its distinguished constellation of voices have been gathered together in one place. Here you will find Martha Stewart and Cindy Crawford holding forth on perfection, Donatella Versace and Jay McInerney speaking about indulgence, Deepak Chopra on epiphanies, Yoko Ono on patience, Sarah Jessica Parker on transformation, Neil deGrasse Tyson on the future—even Miss Piggy on love. The format allows these luminaries to break free of the constraints of conventional interviews or Q&As, providing a space for deeply personal reflections and resurfacing anecdotes and insights that are often a key to understanding what made them who they are today.

The range of perspectives is inspirational. I was as tickled by David Sedaris's reflections on willpower ("I have to overdo pretty much everything") as I was edified by Kenneth Branagh's observation that ambition has given him "tremendous energy and a way of looking at the world." Diane von Furstenberg offers a highly personal take on independence, while the late architect Zaha Hadid opened up about her philosophy of design. On the subject of discipline, Karl Lagerfeld is charmingly blunt: "Discipline? Oh, I have none."

There is no right or wrong way to read this book. Some may decide to follow the pages sequentially from start to finish, to absorb the many crosscurrents of thought that emerge. Others will prefer to dip in at a random spot for a daily dose of inspiration. Two indexes at the back of the book—one listing the columnists alphabetically by name, another cataloging the topics discussed—are another point of entry. So whether you're looking for words of wisdom from Tory Burch, Questlove, Simone Biles or Jonathan Franzen, or you're after a primer on risk, habit, innovation or loyalty, you've come to the right place.

I hope you get as much enjoyment out of the book as we have putting it together for you.

Kristina O'Neill, April 2018

THE COLUMNISTS

CHERYL STRAYED

ON ADVICE

"Some people have a negative reaction to the word *advice*. They imagine somebody shaking their finger and telling them what to do. That kind of advice is never helpful. Good advice is simply about sharing your perspective. When I started writing an advice column, I approached it with a sense of curiosity and a light heart, and I quickly realized that it was incredibly meaningful work. I was using stories to illuminate those deeper human truths that can so often be guiding lights for us. The big questions were always about love, sex and family. Will I ever be loved? How do I heal when bad things happen? The letters I got could be devastating. But there's something about being able to help others that's empowering. You shift from despair to hope. We are made stronger for our suffering, especially when we turn that into generosity, into helping others."

Strayed is an author.

KENNETH BRANAGH
ON AMBITION

"A few years ago I played the lead in *Macbeth*, a drama about ambition, on the stage—unhealthy ambition, one might say, that carries resentment, aggression, treachery and acquisitiveness. Lady Macbeth says of her husband, 'Art not without ambition, but without the illness should attend it.' But I think this pejorative association with ambition is a dangerous thing. Ambition can give us a sense of purpose, meaning and determination. And I think that ambition need not be ruthless. Ambition begets adventure, a process that teaches us that the journey is potentially more enjoyable than the arrival. Ambition has given me tremendous energy and a way of looking at the world. What I've learned about ambition is to share it, that it need not always be about you, that it works best quietly but insistently and can indeed be healthy, despite what Lady Macbeth says."

Branagh is an actor and director.

ARIANNA HUFFINGTON

ON INTUITION

"Learning to trust my intuition has been a lifelong journey. We have many voices inside us, and we need to learn to distinguish between the voices of wisdom and the voices of fear. Plotinus, the third-century Roman philosopher, said that knowledge has three degrees: opinion, science and illumination. So intuition doesn't mean excluding facts and data—it means adding another powerful source of knowledge. Steve Jobs talked about making room to hear subtle things, to be able to 'listen to the whisperings.' It takes practice: For me, it means meditating, getting enough sleep and being in nature as much as possible. We all need to experiment to find what works for each of us. The common denominator is getting away from the everyday stresses, like putting away our devices and not being connected to the world 24/7—being able to distinguish the noise from the signal."

Huffington is an author, syndicated columnist and businesswoman.

SAMANTHA BOARDMAN

ON DISCIPLINE

"I think of discipline in the context of self-control. For a lot of us, it's hard to imagine anything besides 'I want it, and I want it now.' Picture a hungry toddler banging on the table waiting for dinner. Impulsive behavior is appealing: In the heat of the moment, you want that piece of cake or that pair of shoes, but you are not thinking about the consequences. Instant gratification can lead to trouble. Self-discipline is not just about temptation; it's also about our own emotions and reactions. It's important to have enough self-discipline to hit the pause button and appraise a situation. It's about not reacting to the latest and the loudest, but instead thinking about your future self. For example, if you don't pay your bills, you won't be able to get credit. That's where habit comes in; you have to train yourself—it's almost like building a muscle. Self-discipline reminds us we always have a choice. If you are willing to explore alternative behaviors, you open yourself up to possibilities that you never dreamed of."

Boardman is a psychiatrist at Weill Cornell Medical College.

MARY J. BLIGE

ON INDULGENCE

"I have a thing for Lorna Doone cookies, a kind of love affair going on with them. Even if I'm full, I need to have at least five Lorna Doone cookies, which is not cool, but I've got to have them. And I don't even want to go into ice cream. Me and ice cream, we have a thing too. It's important to reward yourself. There have been times when I've had no vacation, just working, working, working, but you're not actually making any real progress because you're not taking care of yourself, not giving yourself a break to regenerate. People tell me my music acts as an indulgence for them, like food for the soul—they say, 'I need Mary right now; this Mary song is hitting the spot.' My song 'Just Fine' celebrates indulgence because at the end of the day, everything is all right, it's just fine. And 'Family Affair' is straight-up indulgence—it's all about fun. Everything can't be serious, you've got to have balance."

Blige is a singer-songwriter.

GEORGE R. R. MARTIN
ON POWER

"Power struggles seem to be omnipresent in every field of human endeavor, extending all the way up and down society. We assume that power has a certain reality. Apart from comic books, where Superman has the power to fly, the only power real human beings have is the power they think they have. You see that sometimes in the collapse of a society. Why did the Soviet Union fall? Because one day the Kremlin gave orders and the soldiers said no, and the whole thing fell apart. It's a fundamental truth that I think Gandhi and Martin Luther King Jr. hit on, that power depends on the obedience of the less powerful. A leader is powerful only when he says jump and people jump. He has no actual power to make them jump. It's their belief that he has power. It's an illusion, a shadow on the wall. And sometimes people stop jumping, and then the world changes."

Martin is a novelist.

TORY BURCH

ON PATIENCE

"Patience was instilled in me at an early age. My father was one of the most patient people I've ever known. When I would rush things, my mother would always say, 'Tomorrow is a new day.' And my own family life has absolutely made me more patient—you have to be when you're raising three boys. Since I'm generally patient, it helps people around me and keeps everything on an even keel—which is especially helpful when we're preparing for fashion week. As a company, we're also very patient in our approach. We're not in a rush, and we're not afraid to say no. In fact, we say no to many opportunities that come our way. In 2008, we wanted to open a Madison Avenue store and found a location but, after some consideration, decided that the space wasn't right for us, and we would keep looking. Shortly after we made the decision, Lehman Brothers collapsed. Our willingness to be patient and wait turned out to be a blessing."

Burch is a fashion designer and CEO.

SIMONE BILES

ON IMPULSE

"I like schedules. I like knowing exactly what I'm doing and when, but there are times in my personal life when I like to be impulsive. I recently went indoor skydiving—my parents wouldn't let me do it before the Olympics; they didn't want me to get injured. It was my brother's birthday, and we said, 'Let's finally do this.' So we told my parents that we were going out to breakfast, but we went sky-diving instead. It was so exciting. Gymnastics is about perfection, it's about control and choreography, but there's still room to be a bit impulsive. When I was on the Kellogg's Tour of Gymnastics Champions, during one of my routines, I fell. So I had to adjust—I threw in a skill that I had been planning for another section. There are also times when impulsiveness can be bad. The other day, I wanted to get a tattoo of the Olympic rings. Thankfully, I thought, 'No, Simone. Call Mom.'"

Biles is a gymnast and an Olympic gold medalist.

SUSAN LUCCI

ON SECRETS

"I remember talking to Agnes Nixon, who created the character Erica Kane on *All My Children.* I was so lucky to play her for four decades. Agnes said it was important for an audience to be in on the secret before the heroine. It creates a kind of tension. They get invested—they want to know when the secret will be revealed and how the character will respond when it is. And Erica had so many secrets! Drama at its best holds up a mirror to the viewer, and Agnes was a groundbreaker in telling stories that were way ahead of their time. Soaps can get away with it. There was an abortion that Erica wanted to keep secret from her second husband. And then, of course, there was the rape by her father's best friend—it was the secret that drove her. Sometimes, like Erica, we keep secrets because we're simply terrified of how others will react."

Lucci is an actor.

DR. PHIL MCGRAW

ON SECRETS

"Old sayings get to be old sayings because they're profound, like 'The truth will set you free.' Carrying a secret can be draining, and the most toxic secret of all is the one stemming from shame. I grew up with a seriously alcoholic father. When you're in an alcoholic home, you learn about secrets early on. Your whole life is a secret. Everyone has a social mask. We all go out of our house with our faces freshly scrubbed and shiny. We don't go to school and disclose that the utilities were turned off in our house because our father didn't pay the bill. We don't say the window was kicked out of our house because he came home in a drunken rage the night before. The isolation that is involved in secret keeping can erode self-esteem and self-worth. It can kill the soul. But you have to have the courage to disclose those kinds of secrets, to cure yourself of that cancer."

McGraw is a psychologist and the host of Dr. Phil.

SARAH JESSICA PARKER
ON TRANSFORMATION

"I love the process of becoming somebody else, but the work to become so, and to be convincing, is still very challenging. Every project is brand new and scary. People probably don't realize that Carrie Bradshaw was radically different from who I was, who I continue to be. I think that sometimes because we look alike and live in the same city and haunt the same neighborhoods, that it was sort of like I was playing in the sandbox, when in truth it took real work every day to be her, to understand her, to not judge her. I'm working on a series for HBO. The character I'm playing is incredibly different from me in many ways—she handles complexity differently than I do, her marriage is different from my own, and she's struggling financially in a way that I don't at this point in my life. But that's what I love. I still love the idea of being somebody else."

Parker is an actor.

DAVID
SEDARIS
ON WILLPOWER

"The level of my willpower depends on what I'm trying to stay away from. When it came to giving up drugs, cigarettes and alcohol, I felt slightly above average. Ditto the first 10 times I lost weight. Lately though, at least in the dieting department, I'm starting to feel below average. I have breasts now and can feel them jiggling as I run to the ice cream truck. My problem is I have to overdo pretty much everything. I got a Fitbit a few years ago, and even that I overdo. On an average day I walk between 15 and 20 miles. I've walked so much that three of my toenails have fallen off. I get up in the middle of the night and practically have to crawl to the bathroom. I'm crippling myself but I can't stop. My partner, Hugh, does everything in moderation. I don't know if that's willpower or just a healthier level of sanity."

Sedaris is an author and humorist.

NASSIM NICHOLAS TALEB

ON INNOVATION

"If you look at the history of innovation, you discover that the process is
much less intellectual than you might
think. Less rationalistic, in the sense
of being derived from the top down.
Much less dominated by schools. And,
typically, driven entirely by tinkering.
Tinkering is just people doing what
they like to do. The results come and
often they don't even recognize them.
It's not purposeful—often the result
has nothing to do with what people
start with. You look for India, you find
America. If you want a breakthrough,
don't specify where you're going. In
the long run, the more randomness,
the more you're going to be helped.
I have no plan when I wake up in the
morning. I have absolutely zero idea
where I'm going. The minute I'm bored
with something, I move on to something else. Life is too short—I follow
stimuli."

Taleb is a statistician and author.

ANN PATCHETT
ON INNOVATION

"I wouldn't wish any more innovation on fiction than has already arrived. With some things, we try to improve, improve, improve, and then we realize it's not better. I've done that with recipes so many times. You mess and mess with it, making it better, and then you go back and make it the first way again and think, Actually, that tastes a lot better. My dog—nobody's going to improve on this dog. The innovation of the family pet? It's not going to get any better. Bookstores: still absolutely the best way to buy a book. My husband has lots of classical vinyl records, and there are days when I come downstairs on a weekend morning and he's playing Shostakovich, and it's really lovely. You can have the iPod playing while you brush your teeth all you want, but to come into the living room and hear that record on the turntable—it's deep."

Patchett is an author.

CINDY CRAWFORD

ON PERFECTION

"When I was a kid, I hated having a beauty mark. My sisters called it an ugly mark. I got teased about it. When I started modeling, some people would even retouch it out of the photograph. But without it, I'm not sure I would have stood out in the same way. Our imperfections make us who we are. And in my case being memorable was more important than being perfect. On photo shoots, I never think about trying to be perfect. I'm trying to tell a story. It might not be perfection we're after—it might even be slightly harsh or ugly or brazen. I once did a shoot with Helmut Newton in Monte Carlo for *Vogue*: big hair, red lipstick, high heels, a blindfolded string quartet. It was weird, but it felt perfect—it was perfectly Helmut. On another shoot— a cover by Herb Ritts for an Italian women's magazine—I thought, That's the way I want to look when I wake up in the morning. That's the best Cindy. That's the girl, the fantasy version of my natural self."

Crawford is a supermodel, businesswoman and philanthropist.

BRIAN GRAZER

ON FAILURE

"Failure has played the most meaningful role in my life. With my movie about a mermaid, *Splash*, I must have had a thousand people say no to me on that. And they always said no in a way that was kind of degrading, like— what, a mermaid? And so when it worked, I thought, Wow! Nobody knows. Nobody really does know. Because all those people—many of them experts in their own right, running studios or directing movies— said no to me. So I thought, You just need to follow your own truth. I remember seeing Steven Spielberg, after doing *Raiders of the Lost Ark* and *Jaws*, being turned down on *E.T.* And I thought, Wow, this isn't personal. Even Spielberg, this prodigy who has real empirical evidence of being a genius, is being turned down on a movie he loves. That was a signature moment for me. I thought, I just have to keep going."

Grazer is a film and television producer and author.

ROBIN DUNBAR

ON GOSSIP

"The original meaning of the word *gossip* refers to something positive, the idea of hanging over the backyard fence and chatting with your neighbors about pretty much nothing—it's about building relationships with members of your community. But gossip has acquired a secondary, negative meaning as well. Malicious gossip derives from the fact that we like to make sure that our friends and neighbors are toeing the general community line. You have to remember that the kinds of societies that we, as well as our monkey and ape cousins, live in are really a form of social contract. We agree to work together to solve problems for our successful survival. But in order for that to work, we have to be prepared to give up some of our more selfish interests, so having a mechanism like gossip that allows us to police other people's behaviors becomes important."

Dunbar is a professor of experimental psychology at the University of Oxford.

JUDY SMITH

ON GOSSIP

"I don't believe that gossip and the truth are mutually exclusive, but even when gossip is truthful, or semitruthful, it can be counterproductive. As a crisis manager, I've seen families broken apart, reputations torn to tatters. We live in a 24-hour news cycle, and in my work we're always putting out fires—I'm continually surprised by the speed at which gossip moves. But sensation sells. The juicier the gossip, the more readers a story attracts. Facts are becoming obsolete. We always prepare our clients for various scenarios, for the scrutiny of the media spotlight; it's essential they remain focused and avoid paying attention to the other stuff. Professionally, I'm known for my discretion, and this line of work has made me even more sensitive to the value of privacy. I try to remain mindful of that."

Smith is founder and president of Smith & Company, a strategic advisory firm.

MICHAEL MUSTO

ON GOSSIP

"I used to sit on the stoop with my family and the next-door neighbors and dish about others in the neighborhood—what they wore, who they were dating. I was a very shy child who rarely spoke, but I really felt like I'd found my home on that stoop. Gossip was a way to bond with others by the proverbial water cooler. But gossip doesn't only have to be fluff. It also sheds light on profound aspects of human behavior. A lot of times we're learning by negative example—this is how you should not lead your life. The biggest gossip story of the modern age has to be Brad dumping Jennifer for Angelina—in tone, it was almost like a Greek tragedy. You had the matinee idol, the good girl and the temptress. Because, of course, celebrities do everything in a bigger way, including messing up. But there's always the next chapter when they rise up again and we cheer them on."

Musto is a journalist.

LEIGHTON MEESTER

ON GOSSIP

"I've never lived for gossip, but I get it. It's only human to want a little bit of something that's bad for you, whether it's chocolate or alcohol or a piece of juicy gossip. But, like anything, gossip in excess can become increasingly addictive. To some extent, gossip is pleasurable for the very same reasons we enjoy watching movies and TV—it's a fantasy of sorts, a close-up look at someone else's life. But it's important not to get too caught up in what's said about *you*—especially if it's coming from people you don't know, because they only see one small side, the side you choose to present. It can be really hard on women, particularly for women in the public eye. You might begin to nitpick your looks or your personality. That's why it's essential to surround yourself with a warm, nonjudgmental circle."

Meester is an actor.

GEORGE SAUNDERS
ON PROCRASTINATION

"Procrastination has a psychological component; there's something you're trying to avoid. I spent most of my 20s procrastinating instead of writing, because I was afraid that if I started I'd find out that I wasn't any good and I'd have to go to law school or something. But over time I got comfortable with the idea of revision. I began to understand that the first draft is usually going to be crummy. I talk about this to my students, who are wonderful young writers. There is a tremendous struggle ahead for them. They must come to grips with their talents, and their anti-talents; they must figure out what they can do uniquely—and that's really hard. There are a lot of offramps, some that you can't even help. I tell them, I understand that it hurts to get critiqued in workshop, but it's important to try to get in relation to that criticism so that you can process it intelligently and benefit from it."

Saunders is an author.

DIANE VON FURSTENBERG

ON INDEPENDENCE

"Independence is the most important thing in my life. My mother was in the Nazi concentration camps when she was 20, so she was a prisoner of the worst kind. She survived, and I was born afterwards in America.
She taught me that fear is not an option and that the most important thing was to be independent. I found my independence through the business of fashion, and through my wrap dress I was able to share that independence and confidence with a lot of women.
I lived the American dream. I believe women need to have children, but they also need to have an identity outside of family. I felt the least independent when I wasn't working, like I had lost my identity. Women are afraid of their own strength. But we have more independence than ever now—we forget how much we have achieved."

Von Furstenberg is a fashion designer.

GAVIN BROWN

ON COLOR

"Color is a reality. The white spaces of a contemporary art gallery are only a social convention—one that will inevitably be replaced by yet another convention of a different kind. Color is in everything. It is everywhere, equally: in the whitest gallery and in the grayest bank. Color in galleries is to be expected, but if I were to choose, I prefer the colors I find in my everyday life. I like the colors in flags. I like the colors in money, the color of cars, of sheets, of magazines all in a row at Hudson News at the airport. I like the different colors of credit cards in a wallet. I like the color of candy wrappers, I like the color of terrorist-threat alerts, I like the colors of Republicans and Democrats. I like the color of rubber tires. These are colors that talk to me eye to eye. Someone chose them for me. They are there to be looked at as much as a painting. Art is everything we make—everything we see and everything we name. And that includes color. Color of any kind."

Brown is owner of Gavin Brown's Enterprise, an art gallery.

JOHN BALDESSARI
ON COLOR

"When I was a painter, I believed in relational color; that is: This color goes nicely with that color. After I left painting in the late '60s, I began exploring photography, and merging painting and photography into a hybrid. Since then I've used color as a signal. Red equals danger, green equals safety, etc. While these are not universal meanings, it does help me escape relational color. Central to my work is absence, and when I omit part of an image, that part is painted white. My favorite color is blue, but I guess that's everybody's favorite color. An art dealer once told me that people avoid paintings with purple in them, and he has to discount them by 20 percent. The door of my house is painted orange so visitors can find it—another example of color as signal. The only mistake with color that I have regretted is once crossing an intersection against a red light. I almost got killed."

Baldessari is an artist.

CARINE ROITFELD
ON PERSUASION

"Honestly, I don't like the word *persuasion*. It's quite aggressive. I think *seduction* and *suggestion* are better words. Politicians have the gift of persuasion. As a stylist I never want to push someone to do something, because they may regret it in the end. When I worked with Kim Kardashian on the cover of *CR Fashion Book*, with Karl Lagerfeld and Riccardo Tisci, she was not heavily supported by the fashion world. We wanted her with no hairstyling and makeup, which was very different for her. The result was a totally new vision of her—although, of course, it's easy to persuade people when you're working with Karl and Riccardo! And a sense of humor always helps. But I think we have to accept that these days not everyone can be persuaded. The work I did 20 years ago would be very difficult to do today."

Roitfeld is a stylist and the founder and editor-in-chief of CR Fashion Book.

JEFF KOONS
ON HABIT

"In my day-to-day life I am a person of habit. I come to the studio every day around 8:30 a.m. and I leave around 5:30 p.m. I have a strict diet—every day I have the same amount of pistachios and the same amount of Cheerios and I'll eat two Zone bars throughout the day. I try to be right on the edge of getting the exact best proportion of fats, carbs and protein. I enjoy the discipline, and it lets me not really have to think about my diet, so I can think about other things. I train five days a week at lunchtime between noon and 1 p.m. I have a gym at my studio and I go there for one hour, and it lets me forget about everything else. When it comes to my work, I would say that my process, the way I go about starting to think about a work, is the same—I just follow and focus on my interests."

Koons is an artist.

KENDALL JENNER

ON YOUTH

"I feel like I grew up too fast a long time ago. Having older siblings, you grow up around adults, so you mature more quickly. I saw my sisters and parents working every day, so I was pretty much brought up to be a workaholic. But I turned 20 not too long ago, and it was a little scary—it's the first step out of being a teenager. My sister Khloé always says to me and my younger sister, Kylie: You have your whole life to be an adult but only so long to be a kid. And we get it. In the right situations, I try to be as immature as I can sometimes—react to things as if I were 12. You can't take things too seriously. I just laugh thinking about my dad being a teenager, partying. It's the funniest thing. And it makes me think—what am I going to be like when I'm 65?"

Jenner is a model.

WYLIE DUFRESNE
ON THE FUTURE

"In food, I think in a way we're coming to the end of the railroad track. We've ridden what's been laid before us, and our duty is to continue laying more track. The track has to go on—it's not going to end, but we're not necessarily sure where it's going to go. I hope that when the score is tallied up, we [at wd~50] will have contributed a decent amount of track and been a part of the avant-garde. But I've never been much of a futurist—I'm not trying to channel my inner Buck Rogers. I'd say I'm more of a modernist; we're not trying to anticipate trends. My sense of the future is actually in some ways very short term. Life as a cook is about the immediate future. It's not about next year; it's about, 'How am I going to get through these 12 hours—and come out on the plus side?'"

Dufresne is a chef.

ANNE WOJCICKI
ON THE FUTURE

"I was brought up with a scientific outlook on life. It's the way my father deciphers the world—whether it's football, politics or hairstyles. So I don't get anxious about the future, because I was raised to believe and accept that nothing stays the same, and the best way to survive is to adapt. I have faith in humanity that society will, over time, make the right decisions and evolve. I believe that we all have freedom to shape our own life and the world around us. One of the things that got me interested in genetics was the relationship between genes and environment. We are all dealt a certain deck of cards, but our environment can influence the outcomes. The fact that my environment influences my life so much— and that my environment is in my control—gives me a great sense of empowerment over my health and my life."

Wojcicki is a biologist and the cofounder and CEO of 23andMe.

NEIL DEGRASSE TYSON

ON THE FUTURE

"In the 1950s and '60s, thinking about the future was a major pastime. We were headed to the moon, and everyone knew it required advanced science and technology. Dreams were put on the table and then realized. Everything was 'of tomorrow.' That pastime has evaporated. We're getting excited about the next app, but that's different from awaiting revolutions in technology. I don't tend to value-judge, but if we stop dreaming about the future, then tomorrow is much more likely to be the same as today. In the 20th century, Americans led the world in major inventions. But the ambitions of the nation have flatlined. You go through the school system and come out on the other side, and there's no grand vision to walk into. To get everyone thinking about the future again may require another big project where we dream the impossible dream and achieve the impossible goal."

Tyson is an astrophysicist and author.

ALAN CUMMING

ON STYLE

"I think it's really important to have your own style as an actor. It has nothing to do with fashion—having an idiosyncratic style is about self-knowledge, a level of comfort with yourself and how you project yourself to the world. It makes you identifiable and unique. Sometimes I wear things that I know are going to upset people. I do it on purpose. I'm comfortable enough to be provocative and to sort of charge people not to take it too seriously. So as an actor, having a public identity and a unique sense of style makes it really interesting, because when you add a character on top of yourself, it gets sort of Brechtian: You're asking the audience to step outside the situation and see both you and the character you're playing. On *The Good Wife*, I think people liked my character as much for what he did as for the fact that they knew it was me playing him. Good or bad, I am who I am."

Cumming is an actor.

RUTH REICHL
ON TASTE

"The thing that's so interesting about taste to me as a writer is that, when you look at something, we all know that we're pretty much seeing the same thing. With sensation, we're pretty sure that when we touch a rough thing, we're feeling the same thing. But none of us has any idea if we're tasting the same taste. It's an incredibly abstract concept. Taste is the most mysterious sense—scientifically they're still not entirely sure how it works. We have a very limited vocabulary to describe it. My goal as a restaurant critic was to try and have people sitting at the table with me. I realized early on that I had to get beyond too much salt, too little sugar, and that I had to do a kind of synesthesia for people: Tell them it's like running through a field, or compare it to music. The wonder of taste is that it's more than just flavor in your mouth. It's an all-encompassing experience."

Reichl is a food writer, novelist and editor.

BART
SIMPSON
ON VIBES

"Vibes are what I see in my dad's stomach when he jumps up and down. There are lots of bad vibes at school, although it may be because the building is not to code. I'm good at picking up on bad mojo and guessing if I'm in trouble, because frankly I always am. The vibes I get from girls are: yuck, yuck, double-yuck, yuck, cooties, yuck! My own vibes are on the spectrum of 'rude dude with plenty o' 'tude.' That's why I like skateboard culture, because no one tells you what to do. But I think my vibes have mellowed over the years—I'm not the same angry, disrespectful monster I was when I was 3."

Simpson is a character on the cartoon show The Simpsons.

REGGIE WATTS

ON VIBES

"As a comedian, you definitely pick up on vibes. They give you the general feeling of a situation. You go into a room, and how it feels determines the what, when and how of your performance. I listen to what the comedians who perform before me say about the crowd, and I watch all their acts. On stage, when things are in sync, in resonance, magic things start to occur. Something happens when you feel interconnected—to me, that's our natural state. If you hit a certain note in a room full of people, it raises the whole vibe of the room. Picking up on vibes is definitely about listening, literally listening to everything around you, from an idea floating around in your head to what's physically around you. I try to listen to the ineffable, the intangible. Everything has its own vibrations."

Watts is a comedian, musician and bandleader.

LARRY WILMORE

ON WIT

"Someone slipping on a banana peel is funny, but there's nothing witty about it. Wit involves using language in a clever way to reveal some greater truth. We appreciate both the cleverness and the light that it shines for us. In my comedy, I love tackling dangerous racial or social situations, using language in a way to disarm them. The first show I ever created was called *The PJs*—we used to push the envelope all the time. I mean, we had a character who was a crackhead! Once, we had two kids talking to each other and one said, 'I hope we never grow old,' and the other kid said, 'Well, the statistics are in our favor!' That's a *hard* joke, but that line would be relevant today. I would rather defend an uncomfortable truth than be defending something that's simply done for shock value."

Wilmore is a comedian, writer, producer and actor.

ROZ
CHAST

ON WIT

"In my cartoons, I prefer funny to
witty; I go for something that makes
the reader laugh. When I think of wit, I
imagine watching a television show
with too much repartee. I can sense the
writers' room behind the conversation.
People don't talk like that. It just feels
mechanical to me, and I register it in
an intellectual way but it doesn't make
me laugh. But funny is something else.
I don't think of Louis C.K. as
necessarily witty, for example, but
simply as somebody who is very
observational and hilariously
funny—the same with Larry David. I
don't think of them as standing back
with one eyebrow raised and saying
exactly the right remark at the right
time. They're just very astute. I love
making myself laugh. I'm sort of
surprised by it every time it happens."

Chast is a cartoonist.

NAOMI CAMPBELL

ON CONFIDENCE

"Before I go to walk on a catwalk, I am nervous. I may not show it, but I am nervous, always. I say a little prayer and cross myself before I step out in front of people. It's never planned what I'm going to do when I get out on the runway. I try to use my nerves to overcome and to make me do a good job. I always say, 'Fake it till you make it.' You can use fear or insecurity to get you over. It's a positive, actually; it's not a negative at all. Once, I fell down in Vivienne Westwood. There's a technique to walking in her big platforms—you go in on your toe—but I was walking like I was wearing regular shoes, and I went down. I said, 'OK, I'm down,' I picked myself up and kept going. If you carry yourself like you have confidence, you could actually have it or you could not, but we'll never know, will we?"

Campbell is a supermodel.

JUDITH LEIBER

"I was born in Budapest. In addition to Hungarian, we spoke German at home. My sister and I also learned English as young girls because in order to go to Western Europe you had to learn the languages—English, French, Italian, Spanish. I eventually went to school in London and spoke English well enough to register to study chemistry. But I never got to because shortly after I returned to Hungary, in 1939, the war broke out and I was confined to a Jewish ghetto throughout the Nazi occupation. I left after World War II, ultimately coming to the United States, eager to learn the American way. As I began designing and selling handbags, my fluency in English was incredibly valuable, especially when working with retailers. Even then, I understood that the use of superlatives was crucial to making products as attractive as possible. Although, of course, the beauty of objects is a language of its own."

Leiber was a handbag designer.

PIERCE BROSNAN
ON LANGUAGE

"I've been an immigrant all my life, so I'm quite versed in the language of assimilation. In 1964, when I was 11, I moved from Ireland to London. To be Irish during that period meant you were an outsider. My pronunciation of words was humiliatingly self-evident on the first day of school when I pronounced the *th* in *thirty* differently. I suppose that was my first performance, the burying of a dialect so that I could be part of the community. Later, when I came to the United States, I played with a mid-Atlantic twang because the South London accent I'd developed was not becoming to the image I had in my head. I felt like a fraud, but language was also a vehicle for self-exploration. I have different voices now—Irish, English and American—and I use them to great advantage to be a part of the milieu. They all have different vibrations and different meanings to my life."

Brosnan is an actor.

CAMILLE PAGLIA

ON OPTIMISM

"Exuberant, can-do optimism is the key American mode. I detest morbidly world-weary European affectations, like the cynical postmodernism that flooded American academe in the 1980s. In college during the delirious 1960s, I rejected Samuel Beckett's *Waiting for Godot* as a self-indulgent paean to the doom and gloom of post-Nazi Paris. It's no accident that the bleak *Godot* remained canonical for mandarins like Michel Foucault and Susan Sontag. The sunnily optimistic overkill of the Doris Day–Debbie Reynolds era needed an antidote, but we already had it in beat poetry, with its gritty street populism. Secularists may squirm, but central to American optimism is the evangelical tradition, whose religious revivals countered lingering New England Calvinism. The thunderous hymns of American gospel choirs are inspirational folk art, vanquishing Europe's exhausted elitism."

Paglia is a social critic and author.

MASSIMO BOTTURA

ON LIMITS

"I see limits as opportunities to create something special—it just depends on your perspective and what you think is possible. Think about 'Oops! I Dropped the Lemon Tart,' a dessert at my restaurant Osteria Francescana, which was conceived after my pastry chef Taka dropped a lemon tart he had prepared. He was so upset. I said, 'Listen, you're human. Let's rebuild this imperfection in a perfect way.' Every other chef in the world who dropped a lemon tart would throw it out, but that was unacceptable to me, so we came up with this 'smashed' lemon tart. Some critics have called me an artist, but I'm not an artist—I'm an artisan obsessed with quality. But I like the idea of an artist because he is free to do whatever he wants. Think about Duchamp. The limit? Who knows? But for me an overripe tomato and some bruised zucchini can be an incredible opportunity."

Bottura is a chef.

MARIO SORRENTI

ON OBSESSION

"When I shot the Obsession campaign for Calvin Klein in the '90s, I was going out with Kate [Moss], and we were fairly young. We were really in love. All the guards are down when you're with somebody you completely trust, which led to these incredibly intimate photographs. I think Calvin recognized in my photos a sort of darker, deeper mood. I had this raw thing I was trying to achieve with my images. To me, the pictures of Kate were a declaration of love, but other people took them in a different way. I remember we were trying to find a soundtrack for the commercial, and I ended up going into a recording studio and talking about how I felt about Kate and added some hard, ambient sounds. When that was edited together with all the imagery, it did end up feeling a bit obsessive and crazy. But at the time I was just trying to hold on to something very precious."

Sorrenti is a fashion and art photographer.

BAZ
LUHRMANN

ON LOVE

"Romantic love can be dangerous.
Look at *Romeo and Juliet*. It was
originally written as a cautionary tale:
When kids fall in love, it can end
tragically. It's about kids who are
experiencing love hormonally for the
first time. You throw in a generational
conflict and everybody's walking
around with swords, it's inevitable
that you'll end up with dead children.
People invade countries over love.
Despots—Alexander the Great,
Napoleon—rampaged throughout the
world because the more love they got,
the less they felt they had. If you think
of the great love stories—*Casablanca,
Gone with the Wind, Gatsby*—none of
them end with the boy and girl kissing
and riding off into the sunset. They all
share a fundamental impossibility.
It can never be, but wasn't it grand to
experience? Because the one thing
about intense romantic love is, good or
bad, you feel very, very alive."

Luhrmann is a film director.

JOHN
RIDLEY
ON ADVICE

"I had the opportunity to work with Francis Ford Coppola very early in my career. He told me a story about the film *Patton* [which he co-wrote] that stuck with me. There's a scene where Patton stands in front of a flag addressing troops that you never see—it's a scene that has become iconic in terms of cinema and culture. But Coppola had to fight the studio to keep it in because they just didn't understand it. He told me that the things you have to fight hardest for are the things you'll be remembered for *because* they're so different. I always thought that was an amazing piece of advice. But that was coming from Francis Ford Coppola! I'll readily admit that as a younger person I wasn't always good at accepting advice. Advice is the easiest thing to dispense and the hardest thing to absorb. Hopefully, with a bit of maturity, you can accept those things that might make a difference in your career and life."

Ridley is a writer and director.

PATRICK
WHITESELL
ON ADVICE

"In our business, the ability to give good advice consistently has a direct impact on our capacity for success. Our clients have their own unique careers and objectives. But even though they're on different journeys, they all want a career that provides them with creative fulfillment and happiness. Our job is to get them there. Sometimes they may not agree with our advice or want to hear it—but it's still our responsibility to share that with them. Technology has disrupted the entertainment business since radio, but access to information— especially via social media—is so overwhelming now. The megaphone is bigger, the opinions louder than ever. It creates this confusing environment. A trusted source of advice is critical amid all the noise."

Whitesell is a talent agent and co-CEO of WME-IMG.

AMY CAPPELLAZZO
ON ADVICE

"There's a moment of incredible clarity when you hear the right advice. A light goes on in your head. I consider a few things when advising clients about collecting art, including their station in life and their ultimate goals for the collection—whether they plan to give to the local museum, for instance. I always try to save them from making any catastrophic mistakes. If anything, I'm probably too honest and direct at certain moments. Sometimes I'll say, 'Look, you're rich. You can have anything that you want, but this isn't something you should need that badly. Take a walk around the block.' Part of advice is protecting people from what they want. I feel good when the right object has found the right home. It's a little bit like arranging love when you've made that match."

Cappellazzo is a chairman at Sotheby's and an art adviser.

DIANE REHM

ON LOYALTY

"Loyalty is a two-way street. It really does go both ways—in friendship, family and love. I was married to my husband for 54 years, until his death. I mean, talk about loyalty and kindness—we always supported one another. I remember once, years ago, I became so upset with a co-worker at WAMU that I left the office and drove to the grocery store to clear my mind. The store was near the radio station but about two miles from home. I got to the store but I was so distracted that I lost my car keys. I was hysterical. I called my husband, crying. He knew instantly why I was upset, so he said he'd take a cab immediately. Well, about 20 minutes later, John Rehm walked in. He said nothing; he just put his arms around me and held me. He'd had trouble getting a taxi so he'd walked all the way to the store with my keys. That's what loyalty is—a crucial ingredient in any marriage."

Rehm is an author and the host of
The Diane Rehm Show.

CHAN MARSHALL

ON SOLITUDE

"There are three different solitudes I
love. There's the solitude of the beach,
like the Injidup beach in western
Australia. I was there by myself once,
and instinctively took off my clothes
and went swimming. That's one of the
happiest times I can remember. Then
there's the solitude of the woods or
fields, like near our house when I was
12. I used to go down by the creek and
just be alone—that's my favorite place
ever. And then there's the solitude of
the desert. Being alone, stepping out in
the morning when your friend's still
asleep, and you're stuck out in the
middle of nowhere. You see a hawk and
rattlesnake tracks. There's nothing
and nothing and nothing, and it just
feels so comfortable. And familiar.
You've never been there before, but it's
like, oh yeah, this is a place I love, it's
undoubtedly part of me somehow. That
kind of solitude is available, but you
have to go really far away for it."

*Marshall, also known as Cat Power, is a
musician.*

BUZZ
ALDRIN
ON SOLITUDE

"I'm uncomfortable with solitude. I have a tendency toward negativity— I'm liable to start thinking about all the bad things in my life. In solitude, you start to procrastinate. You think about fairness and unfairness. But I didn't feel alone in space. I felt a part of and in contact with an extended team with a higher problem-solving capability. One thing that can bring on solitude is long durations of flight in space. I'm not a good candidate for that. I'm a sprinter. I like to drive fast, and I'm socially interactive. Teamwork and leadership, I know what they are. On Apollo 11, neither Neil [Armstrong] nor I had the option of returning alone except as an absolute extreme. If you're the person who won't make it back, your partner is probably not going to abandon you. But there may come a time when you'll just run out of oxygen, pass out. Should he wait around for that to happen? No! We had to be prepared to face the solitude of a situation beyond our control."

Aldrin is an author and former astronaut.

KRISTEN SCHAAL

ON LUCK

"It's easy as a comedian to see the world pessimistically. But I've always said that the luckiest people are the ones who can recognize that they're lucky. A lot of people have so many blessings but they won't even be aware of it because they're so focused on what they don't have. I always try to check myself and go, Wow, you're so lucky. I once had a bike accident where I flipped over my bike and landed right on my mouth and broke some of my teeth. It felt like that was really bad luck. It pummeled me in such a big way. But then it also really showed me how wonderful my husband is, and then I thought about getting these teeth that were a little whiter than my old teeth, and I think it turned out to be a pretty lucky thing in the end! You have to put a positive spin on things, don't you? You're lucky when you know you're lucky."

Schaal is a comedian and actor.

DEEPAK CHOPRA

ON EPIPHANIES

"You have a certain set of relationships and you have a story; but suddenly, something can change and you have a new story. At 32, I was a doctor practicing medicine. I saw how people responded unpredictably to treatment. Two people could have the same illness, see the same doctor and still have different outcomes. One day I had an epiphany that body and mind were one. It was startling because I hadn't been trained like that. I faced huge opposition from the mainstream. But you don't have to motivate yourself to follow through on an epiphany; you do it anyway because you're inspired. Motivation, instead, is a result of wanting to transform. I want to lose weight so I'm going to motivate myself to go to the gym—it doesn't work! After 15 days the gym gets my membership fee, and I'm not going anymore. But with epiphanies, there's no going back. "

Chopra is an author and public speaker.

ZAHA HADID

ON DESIGN

"I don't perceive things as a concept of design, but, rather, as architecture. I'm influenced by many elements: In the early years, Russian avant-garde and abstraction, and since then it's varied from topography, geology and computing. But for me what defines good design is something new and refreshing. From there I analyze: Does it function? The biggest mistake is to badly replicate something from the past, like a Baroque building. It will never be as good. In the last 30 years we've made enormous strides into spatial invention, material and technology, which has given a rich period in architecture. Using innova-tive techniques, architects can always create interesting work. I like the Seagram Building, the work of Oscar Niemeyer and the China Central Television headquarters in Beijing. In our work, there is a synergy between the exterior and interior. They are not two separate worlds."

Hadid was an architect.

TOM DIXON

ON DESIGN

"There isn't any point to designing something unless you're making it a bit better than it was before. Good design is just improvement, to pick a single word. It could be a minimal improvement, like a nicer color. Or it could be a much more important improvement, like making something cheaper to manufacture. The LED lightbulb, for example, is fascinating to me as an engineering innovation and a design innovation. What interests me deeply is the collision of digital technology and manufacturing today. You can draw something on-screen and get it made straight from your laptop. It's going to completely change the conversation about where people design and make things. The history of the entire modern industrial world is really about production going to the lower-cost economies. While we still design things, we don't make them anymore. But I think it's going to come back. It's going to be a good thing to design, make and consume things locally again."

Dixon is an industrial designer.

NERI
OXMAN

ON DESIGN

"Like a mathematical axiom, good design is timeless. It transforms the dimensions of life into measures of living. A chair is designed to support our body, but it can also modify our posture by challenging our position in space; the form of a shoe inspires the way we move; the shape of a spaceship defines how (and even why) we conquer outer space. Good design has the power to predict the future, at times through failure. Charles and Ray Eames and Eero Saarinen's inability to construct the first Lounge Chair Wood prototypes originated a new technology for molding plywood. In that, good design reflects the culture that created it. I like to think of design as a state of mind rather than a vocation. It helps to let go of the preconceptions of what it means to be human in order to redefine it."

Oxman is a professor at the MIT Media Lab.

PETER
MARINO

ON DESIGN

"I first understood design at age 3. My mom was changing my curtains and showed me two samples. She said, 'Do you want plaid or stripes?' I thought, Wow, these are the decisions you make in life. I picked the plaid. Today, I'm a functionalist and cannot consider anything to be good design if it doesn't work. The National Library of France in Paris was all glass, and they had to put plywood on the inside of all the windows because the sunlight shone through onto all of the old books. Design has to function. Global architecture also has to account for the local culture. Coco Chanel's original Paris apartment has Coromandel screens and was incredibly exotic. But when we built the first Chanel store in China, we realized that using them would be the least exotic thing to the Chinese. They want something French. You have to consider somebody's values."

Marino is an architect and designer.

MARY-LOUISE PARKER
ON ENVY

"Envy is the demon spawn of self-loathing and comparison. But when you compare yourself to others, you're never going to win. There will always be someone prettier, someone smarter, someone kinder. But it's that comparison that's a slippery slope. On my personal laundry list of shortcomings, envy would not be toward the top, because I'm only ever in competition with myself and my own standards, which I'll never live up to—I don't believe that anything is ever finished or good enough. And envy is always a secret. People hold it close to the vest. Even if you can read all over someone's face that they're envious of someone else, they're never going to come out and admit it, since envy is a great source of shame. And the shame in turn feeds the envy, because to admit that you're envious is to admit to feelings of being lesser."

Parker is an actor.

T. BOONE PICKENS

ON SUCCESS

"Being born in Holdenville, Oklahoma, I didn't have a lot to compare to as far as success was concerned. There was pressure from my family to be successful, but there was no design to it other than to work hard. And everything will come together if you do. I had a paper route when I was 12, and I always had money. I liked that feeling. Everything's been relatively simple for me throughout my life. I saw what happened when you did work—you got results. Now I've given away a billion dollars, and I can't remember a time when I've wanted something I couldn't have. The work ethic that was instilled in me I still have now. I'm in my late 80s, and I'm at the office every day before 8 a.m. I can't imagine retiring. I'm busy. I work out with a trainer every morning. People ask him, 'What's your job?' He says, 'Keeping Mr. Pickens alive.'"

Pickens is founder and chairman of the hedge fund BP Capital Management.

YAEL COHEN BRAUN

ON SUCCESS

"Attitude is a huge part of success. If you don't first believe in yourself, why should anyone else? On the flip side, we millennials, as a generation, have a kind of arrogance—we all want to be entrepreneurs, which sounds so glamorous. We want to own our work. There's so much freedom of choice and so many options today that there's almost a burden of opportunity, whereas in generations past you picked your job and that's what you did. We're all about reinventing the wheel. And when there's a wheel that needs to be reinvented—hell yeah, go for it. But often, joining someone else's team and working with them can be so much more valuable. We have to look at the success we can create together, instead of always wanting to own what we're doing. If people hadn't chosen to come and join me, I would just be some lunatic running around swearing."

Braun is the founder of Fuck Cancer, a nonprofit dedicated to cancer prevention.

BEAR GRYLLS

ON RISK

"Risk has been an inherent part of my life for as long as I can remember—from early days growing up as a young boy on a little island off the coast of England and getting rescued by the Coast Guard for foolishly believing I could navigate across the quicksand of our local harbor at low tide to eventually climbing Everest and then seven seasons of *Man vs. Wild*. The many errors and near escapes from parachute failures to crevasse falls have taught me a few fundamental truths about risk. They are as follows: You only get it wrong once; be smart; trust your inner voice; and don't be too proud to back away. The maxim is right: There are bold mountaineers and old mountaineers, but not many old and bold ones! The job of a survivor is simple: Stay alive."

Grylls is an adventurer, writer and television presenter.

STEPHANIE ROBLE
ON STRATEGY

"We look at our general racecourse strategy as, How would we go around the course without any other boats there? But obviously once you factor in 99 other boats, you can't always execute your strategy. So a good tactician is someone who can take that strategy and then analyze what the other boats are doing around them and how they can best stick to that strategy. It's difficult because you have to balance your risk versus your reward. Sometimes, if you're deep in the fleet, you have to be very risky in your tactics and say, We don't have much to lose but a lot to gain. Or if you're in the front you might say, We need to be very conservative here. And going with your gut is very important. We have a saying on one of the boats that I sail on: If your gut is telling you to do something, do it. Because oftentimes other people are thinking the same thing. And if you don't do it, they're going to do it for you."

Roble is a professional sailor.

DANNY MEYER
ON STRATEGY

"There's this fantastic quote from Peter Drucker: 'Culture eats strategy for breakfast.' I spend about 80 percent of my time thinking about the culture of our company—culture *is* our strategy. At our restaurants we teach the motto of 'constant, gentle pressure' to master a world in which there are unexpected and sometimes very challenging variables tossed your way. It's a technique for not getting knocked off your surfboard by the waves that are inevitably going to sneak up behind you. You cannot become a champion surfer in a bathtub. Some competitors are enormously motivated by whom they can beat—they want that knockout punch—while others are motivated by hating to lose. But I don't really like beating other people. What I like to focus on is living up to our potential as a company, beating our own personal best, constantly stretching a little bit further over time."

Danny Meyer is a restaurateur.

DORIS KEARNS GOODWIN

ON STRATEGY

"With strategy, the key thing is the ability to diagnose the opportunity of the time. Both Herbert Hoover and FDR had the Depression, but it was FDR who diagnosed what to do with it: experimentation, get moving, get people into jobs. So it's not only the opportunity that provides something for the man, it's whether the man is able to adapt and diagnose what needs to be done, and then that becomes the strategy. Abraham Lincoln knew how to diagnose the self and figured out ways to learn from failure. He knew he was too soft on issuing pardons to soldiers who ran away from battle, so he made a pact with his war secretary, who was much more tough-minded, so they could veto each other a certain percentage of the time. By having that opposite kind of person around him, someone who was blunt and mean, he formed a team to shore up his weakness."

Goodwin is a historian and author.

JEFFREY EUGENIDES

"The first association I had with vulnerability was from Latin class. The word *vulnus* means wound. We usually encountered it in *The Aeneid* and various epic poems dealing with actual battle and physical wounds. That's one way to think about it. As the term has become popularized, it sort of involves a willingness to show where one is hurt or weak or soft. It's gone from something that might connote weakness to a sort of secret strength— as though in showing where one can be hurt, one gains communication with another. Vulnerability is essential to fiction. In order to go deep in your writing you have to wade into territory that might feel shameful or embarrassing, a state of maximum vulnerability. The paradox is that being a writer also requires invulnerability in that you need to wall yourself off to judgment and criticism. So you have to be both hard and soft, and know when to be each of those things."

Eugenides is an author.

NAN
GOLDIN
ON MEMORY

"My first and primary reason for photographing was all about memory, to record my life in a way that no one else could revise. Now I find that it's the pictures I didn't take that I remember the best—the film that came out black. I think now that photographs are not actually the best way to preserve a memory, because they start to exist as themselves. They're like a story of a story, not necessarily a real memory. I still want to believe that my own photos record my experience honestly. I no longer believe as I used to that pictures by nature are true, given what modern technology makes possible. That said, I took photographs of my father dying two years ago. We were very, very close, and he was 99 years old. When I view those pictures, they're too painful for me to look at. So there are still photos that evoke the same feelings I had when I took them. I can't look at them, but I needed to take them."

Goldin is a photographer.

THELMA
GOLDEN
ON MEMORY

"I live and work in Harlem, a place where my father was born in 1926. We have conversations now that are built on the foundation of his memories of this neighborhood that are matched with my dreams and aspirations for Harlem. So we exist in this kind of place together where he has an incredibly beautiful, vivid hold on the past but he also has experience of the potential future as I talk about the work that we are doing here at the museum. It's interesting because it points to how someone else's memories can become your own, even in small ways. There are many streets that have changed their names in Harlem. Generationally, I exist within those new names, but I speak the old ones often because that's the memory that he lives in: That's what this was, that's what this is going to be. Memory is an active process of connection."

Golden is the director and chief curator of the Studio Museum in Harlem.

ALEX TREBEK

ON MEMORY

"*Jeopardy!* is basically a memory game. It's stuff you have learned in your life that you have to be able to recall quickly under pressure. Not everyone is able to do it. People ask me all the time, do you remember the information, the clues? Unless it's an area of interest to me, it's in one ear, out the other. It's not so much the facts that I remember as the people: Ken Jennings losing on his 75th show; the first blind contestant, Eddie Timanus, winning on his fifth show; the staff I've worked with here. Emotionally, those memories just resonate, and those are the things that are most important. Having said all that, I think I'm a year and a half younger than Mark Twain was when he died. He had a great comment about that time in his life along the lines of, 'I used to remember everything, but now I only remember the things that never happened.' That's kind of where I'm at."

Trebek is the host of Jeopardy!

FRAN LEBOWITZ
ON MANNERS

"When you speak to people of my generation, you'll find that our parents didn't talk to us about things; they just told us what to do. From morning until night, you were issued instructions. Seventy-five percent of those instructions had to do with manners—don't reach in front of another person, elbows off the table. As a result, you had a certain way of seeing the world. I went to the Nobel Prize ceremony with Toni Morrison the year she won. I got up at one point during the dinner to talk with the wife of an editor at Knopf. But when I got to her, she practically shoved me to the ground and said, 'Don't you know you can't stand up when the king is sitting down?' Well, no, I didn't know that. How would I know that? Of all the things my mother told me, that is one thing she missed. But other than that I pretty much know everything!"

Lebowitz is a writer and social commentator.

FRED ARMISEN

ON TIMING

"Comedic timing is a matter of a million things going the right way. There's not a whole lot you can do to calculate timing. You can do the math as much as you want, and still, it has an equal chance of being funny or not funny. Most comedians have a good sense of timing through practice. But even the best are surprised by how something works one night versus another—there's the mood of the audience, the quality of your voice, the way you're thinking. The element of chance is what makes it fun. It becomes like a sporting event, playing golf or hitting a ball with a baseball bat. There's so little that you can predict. Sometimes timing is built through editing. On *Portlandia*, we did something called 'Did you read it?' When we shot it, we sort of slowly said the lines. The director edited so that some of it was repeated, echoed, and we really chopped it down. The timing lived in the editing."

Armisen is a comedian and musician.

LAURA A. WASSER

ON COMMITMENT

"As a family law attorney, I'm often asked how I can continue to work with people who are going through such terrible times, particularly celebrities in the public eye. But, honestly, my belief in the idea of commitment has only grown stronger since I started practicing. Of course, it gets tiring; it's a challenge to deal with the wearing down of relationships day in and day out. But I also see couples committed to putting their children's needs first, couples able to evolve into a different structure for the good of the family— it's what I saw my parents do when they split up. Many people will tell you that the biggest commitment issue in the demise of a marriage is adultery, but I find that's more symptomatic of a larger problem. People say marriage or parenthood is the hardest job you'll ever do, but the reason we do it is because of the amazing feelings that come back to us as a result of our perseverance, our strength and our commitment."

Wasser is a family law attorney.

ANGELA WESTWATER

ON COMMITMENT

"For a lot of people, the word *commitment* has a financial or legal connotation; for me, it's about emotional or intellectual allegiances. Before I started my gallery, I worked as managing editor of *Artforum* under the leadership of one of the founders, John Coplans. He was tremendously important to me as a mentor. The staff was five people total—it couldn't exist now. I was Ms. Spellcheck and I could typeset. We all did a bit of everything. We were committed to promoting certain issues. There was not, for instance, much of a focus on women artists and feminism in the art world, but that began to change under John— I did plenty of nudging. There were all these issues that arose and in a way stoked my commitment to artists. I witnessed all of John's marvelous friendships and thought, Well, you can have these art relationships too. You can work on their behalf."

Westwater is a founding partner of Sperone Westwater art gallery.

SUSAN MEISELAS
ON COMMITMENT

"I've always been committed to maintaining a connection to subjects who have participated in the making of an image; for me, it's not just about capturing and framing moments in time or people in time, but thinking about them over time and rethinking my relationship to them. That's been very central to my practice as a photographer. I try to frame someone within a moment so that they recognize themselves, a reflection of who they feel themselves to be or what that moment meant. A certain level of commitment can close one down in the sense that if you choose one path you're not on another. The work I did in Kurdistan in the '90s meant that I stayed in one region with one principal motivating idea. I narrated a period of my life through that commitment— it meant I wasn't elsewhere. But all choices have consequences. Commitment is just another way of acknowledging that."

Meiselas is a photographer.

DONATELLA VERSACE
ON INDULGENCE

"Versace will never be minimalist. Versace is about 'more.' That's the way we've been from the beginning, that's the way we'll always be—more, more, more. Our customers are attracted to us because they know that from Versace they will gain the greatest indulgence. Of course, it takes hard work and dedication behind the scenes to make this maximalism look effortless. There's no room for indulgence in the design process. Every single piece has to work, or it has no place in the collection. There are certain elements that will always be part of Versace. We will always show glamorous gowns. Our models will always wear high heels. But these aren't indulgences. They are part of our DNA. Indulgence depends on the individual woman, her lifestyle, her dreams. For some, a bottle of perfume is enough; for others, it is an Atelier Versace gown. My goal is to provide indulgence to all women, whatever their desires."

Versace is the artistic director and vice president of the Versace Group.

JOAN JULIET BUCK

ON OPTIMISM

"Cynicism reduces everything to dark dust. It's reductive and ugly. There are two ways of looking at almost any situation. But it's not always easy. During the AIDS crisis of the '80s and '90s, when so many of my friends were dying, it was very difficult to remain optimistic. But a guiding principle of my life has been something my father, who was given to hyperbole and huge optimism, used to say: 'If nothing is coming to you, do something for someone else.' In times of misery or deep uncertainty, cook for someone. When things are bad, the one thing that you can do—indeed, the only thing that you can do—is focus on the present. I remember when things were really bad for me, I found chives at the Union Square greenmarket in New York that had little blue flowers on them. I had never seen those blue flowers before—they made my day. I went home, made a salad and ate the flowers."

Buck is an author.

DAN
BARBER
ON OPTIMISM

"You could say that a sense of optimism is a requirement for facing many of life's challenges, but I don't know—there are a lot of very highly functional cynical people around. My father, for instance, wasn't imbued with an overriding sense of optimism. And what drives me, even more than optimism, is a fear of failure. Before Blue Hill, I was a chef in a restaurant that slowly went out of business. I didn't even own the place; I lost no money. But the pain of that stays with me. It gets into your marrow. As a father of two young kids, I'm trying to figure this out now: How much do you coddle and imbue them with confidence and a sense of optimism? They're going to have a great deal of realism injected into their lives soon enough. Do you want to be the person to do that or do you want to provide them with a kind of shield? I would love to get an answer!"

Barber is a chef.

BARATUNDE THURSTON
ON INDEPENDENCE

"Independence means nothing without the concept of dependence. Independent from what? In this country, we're fond of the idea of independence being founded in opposition to something. We've got all these legends and myths in America about rugged individualism. There's almost a sense of shame associated with dependence. But dependence is where society comes from, why families stick together, why churches work. Things are shifting, and some of the tools and language of emerging businesses are more about interdependence than independence, but the overall narrative of the country is still very much: We're on our own. Dependence implies trust and sharing and giving. And we're social beings. So there's actually some greatness in dependence and membership. Pursuing extreme independence just for the sake of it doesn't lead to a happy place."

Thurston is an author and comedian.

MARTHA STEWART
ON PERFECTION

"My father was a perfectionist—he was way, way worse than I am—and he taught us the quest for perfection, with any task. If I was laying a cobblestone path for him in the garden, it had to be lined up straight with a string; the stones had to have the exact same amount of space between them. He'd look at it as, how could you lay the path so that it would last forever? I consider myself a teacher, and I think teachers should strive to be perfectionists, in terms of attention to detail and showing the best way possible to do something. I don't expect the consumer to do everything we show them, but if we show them the right way, then they can. There are plenty of very successful people who aren't perfectionists, but then look at the people who are—like Steve Jobs. He was an incredible perfectionist, and his striving for perfection honored what he envisioned. To me, that's amazing."

Stewart is the founder and chief creative officer of Martha Stewart Living Omnimedia, Inc.

CHRISTY TURLINGTON BURNS

ON SUCCESS

"I had what would be considered success really early on in my modeling career. But it wasn't actually a career I thought about or dreamt about. I kind of just fell into it. So while I definitely enjoyed it and appreciated it, it never felt like success, because I didn't really have to work for it. We often think of success as coming at the completion of something, but cliché as it might sound, it's really the doing that's most exciting and rewarding. As we say at Every Mother Counts, the process of carrying and delivering and raising a child has many peaks and valleys. And that's a good thing. Just when it feels like, 'This is such a great moment,' it becomes a difficult moment. I don't think success is supposed to be sustainable, because I don't know that we would enjoy anything if we didn't have ups and downs."

Burns is a model and the founder of Every Mother Counts.

MIKE JUDGE

ON FAILURE

"People in Silicon Valley talk about failure like it's a wonderful thing. They're proud of it to a fault, I think. Because failure really isn't too great. You don't want to fail. There's a lot of luck involved—nobody talks about that much. When they become successful, they go on and on about how they failed and learned from it. But I think there's more luck than people want to admit. A lot of people are big risk takers, but you hear about the ones who won—you don't hear about the ones who went broke and were forgotten. It would appear to the outsider that taking big risks and being willing to fail is the key to success, but I think that's a little misleading. I remember when *Office Space* wasn't doing well at the box office; that one hit me really hard. But eventually I looked at it like, I can handle failure. That's just what you have to do. It's no great wisdom."

Judge is an actor, writer, producer and director.

MINNIE DRIVER
ON MISTAKES

"I genuinely don't believe that mistakes are truly mistakes—I know, it's very 1972 and crunchy. But anything that I've perceived to be a mistake has invariably, at some point down the line, given rise to something else wonderful. I made a movie that was a very difficult experience for everybody, cast and crew. It was nine months in 22 million gallons of water—it wasn't fun. The movie didn't do well. It didn't further my career. It didn't do all the things it was supposed to do. But I couldn't call it a mistake, because so many good things came out of it. I met people during filming whom I'm still friends with today. You have to be aware of the alchemy of life. I think we're too harsh with ourselves about what we consider to be mistakes. The only mistake is looking at your life myopically and not appreciating the vastness of experience."

Driver is an actor.

MARK HADDON

ON CURIOSITY

"In my novel *The Curious Incident of the Dog in the Night-Time*, the main character, Christopher, says something like, 'I think there are enough things in one house to keep you interested for a whole lifetime.' There is deep truth in that. I love the idea that curiosity isn't always about increasing your range or traveling to new places. When I was young, I found biology very boring. I was fascinated by space, as was common with every small boy of my generation. We were all looking up. We were all waiting to land on the moon. But then I began to realize that one of the most exciting frontiers in science was a combination of genetics and cell biology. We think that the most exciting things in the universe happened 14 billion years ago, but the most astonishing things are happening in our fingers. Curiosity is often a case of just looking harder— being open to the world that's immediately around you."

Haddon is an author.

MUSSIE GEBRE

ON CURIOSITY

"As a deaf-blind child, I could not sit back and observe people and events unfolding in front of me. I know my surroundings primarily through the senses of touch, smell and taste. So, for me, curiosity was a means of staying attuned to the world. It was also a way to feel a part of the world of my peers, so that I didn't become the primary object of attention and, possibly, ridicule. Exploring an object or place meant inviting others to join me in the activity and to see me as a curious child, not one to pity because I was different from them. Technology has had a dramatic impact on how I explore the world as an adult. For instance, there are times when I want to know what's going on in town without having to wander around with my guide dog, and the internet empowers me to do just that."

Gebre is president of DeafBlind Citizens in Action.

JOSEPH GORDON-LEVITT

ON CURIOSITY

"I'm a firm believer in the scientific method. That's the great part about science—any conclusion is up for debate. Problems arise when you get too attached to an answer, even in the face of new information or experiences. I find that among the people I know, the most intelligent ones are those who ask questions more than they make statements. They remain curious, even about things they know to be true. There are so many opinions out there, now more than ever, often based on a big game of telephone. The substance of a story can get distorted or reduced to a sound bite—it's what gets retweeted. So I find that if I really want to know something, I have to be curious and make the effort to look into it myself. And acting itself is fundamentally about curiosity—trying to think about a situation other than your own, being someone else."

Gordon-Levitt is an actor.

JULIAN SCHNABEL

ON ESCAPE

"I don't think of *escape* as a pejorative term. Where you escape to is the place that you want to be, rather than the place where you have to confront what people call reality. For me, when I'm painting, one could say that I'm escaping. But what I'm doing is finding a place where I'm more comfortable communicating in a language that is private to me. When I don't feel good or things aren't working out right, I usually paint my way out of it. What you're escaping is the dizziness of anxiety. There's no time and there's no logic other than the logic that exists for the activity you're involved in. It has its own set of rules, so for a while I get a reprieve from a lot of the things that bring me down as an ordinary member of the world. The practice of painting for me is freedom."

Schnabel is an artist.

DAVID DROGA

ON PERSUASION

"The goal of advertising is persuasion and education. Advertisers and brands are primarily asking consumers to give up some of their time, whether it's for a 60-second spot, an online journey or a sponsored event. So it has to be worthwhile and earned. It has to be done with respect. Why should a consumer care about this messaging, be it a phone plan or a pair of sneakers? Persuasion is something that resonates beyond commerce; it functions in all our lives. Everyone is basically an advertiser. If you have an Instagram account, you're essentially running a brand campaign every single day. You're trying to persuade the world that this is the life you lead; these are the ideas you believe in. It's an interesting era. The types of things that prove persuasive change over time, but I think sincerity is the most persuasive quality of all."

Droga is founder and creative chairman of the advertising agency Droga5.

SUSAN N. HERMAN

ON PERSUASION

"True persuasion identifies common ground so that people who may not have expected to agree with you discover that, on some level, they actually do. I gave a talk at the U.S. Army War College a few years ago about ACLU free speech principles. Afterwards, a lieutenant colonel approached me and said he had been determined to disagree with me but was surprised to find that things I'd said made sense to him. Nowadays, there's so much talk about our unbridgeable political divisions— trying to persuade a Democrat to become a Republican or vice versa feels like trying to persuade a tiger to become a vegetarian—but it's dangerous for us to continue retreating into our echo chambers, just to avoid disagreement. I believe that Americans still share many fundamental values, and we need to find ways to listen to each other to persuade ourselves that we can bridge our differences."

Herman is a constitutional law scholar and the president of the American Civil Liberties Union.

SANDRA BERNHARD

ON WIT

"When I think of wit, I think of people like Dick Cavett or Carol Channing. It's like mixing the perfect martini—too much vermouth, and you've ruined it. Wit is dry. It's a touch of self-deprecation and the ability to know when to pull back. You have to be a good listener to be witty. It was second nature in the '60s and '70s—people liked being funny. When I was little, President Kennedy was incredibly witty. I mean, Jack Kennedy could spin a tale. You didn't even know what the hell he was talking about, but you were so taken by his delivery. Everybody wanted to be like that: witty, urbane, sophisticated. Everybody seemed to have that natural ability. To be witty is to be charming. And I think you need to be charming to a certain degree if you're going to have longevity in this business. I've learned to be more charming as the years have gone by. But sometimes I'm just over it."

Bernhard is a comedian and radio host.

ELAINE STRITCH

ON LOVE

"I definitely think of myself as a romantic—without a doubt in the world. I can't believe how romantic I am. It's terrifying! When I saw *Gone with the Wind*, I didn't get out of bed for two days. And Laurence Olivier as Heathcliff in *Wuthering Heights*? That's my idea of romance. And I've had love: Marlon Brando; JFK; Gig Young. I dated them all, but I had such respect for myself. I wanted to hold on to Elaine. At least until I met my late husband, John Bay. It was the first time I felt like, I don't know whether I'm in love or not, but I want to get in his pocket and I want him to take me home. I never talked about sex because I didn't know what the hell that was, but I knew I wanted to be in John's pocket. Being in love is being in somebody's pocket."

Stritch was an actor and singer.

RZA

ON LOVE

"Love is something I've always thought of as the highest elevation of understanding, something that has no conditions to it. Understanding always leads to love. If you love somebody, try to understand them. You may have a couple who love each other, but they don't understand each other. And then the love doesn't live there. Love is a descendant of religion and of reality. It's an equation, like molecules or atoms that combine with other elements. There are many ways to reach that equation, many different expressions of it. The love for your father is different from the love for your wife, or the brotherly love of the Wu-Tang Clan. My love for music has become part of my daily life. There's some things your body has to do every day, and music has become a bodily necessity for me: Every day, I've got to get my fix."

RZA is a musician, actor, director and producer.

MISS
PIGGY
ON LOVE

"Love is when you give yourself totally to another person (or, in moi's case, a frog) and they return the favor—and throw in some expensive jewelry. That said, the very first time I fell in love was when I got my first mirror. I knew that the face looking back at me was one that would woo the world and, with a little Botox, never change. But it's Kermie who truly completes moi. As the saying goes: He had me at 'Hi ho!' Why do I find him so attractive? Look at those spindly arms and legs, that silly little smile, those googly eyes! How could you not fall in love with him? I once went all the way to the Great Swamp in New Jersey to track down Kermit. Wooing is a part of love. I love to woo. I love to be wooed! And sometimes I just like to say the word 'Woo!' My tricks and tips for seduction are easy: I simply hold Kermie tenderly in my arms—and don't let go."

Miss Piggy is a Muppet.

MARGARET ATWOOD

"Envy is one of Shakespeare's major themes. He saw a lot of it around him, mixed in with the power plays of Renaissance politics. In *The Tempest*, for example, Antonio is envious of his brother Prospero's role as duke. Antonio says something like, 'Those fancy clothes, they look just as good on me.' Everything has a positive and negative form. The positive form of envy might be aspirational admiration, the idea that I'm going to try hard to be as good as you. Still, there's a reason envy is one of the seven deadly sins: Instead of working to be as good as you, I'm going to work to *destroy* you. It's very interesting to observe dogs or other social animals, because their place in the hierarchy is important to them. Envy is not just a human thing; it's a very primal thing. Now, how do you keep from letting it consume you? I don't know. Do yoga? Breathe in, breathe out."

Atwood is an author.

MARIA SHARAPOVA
ON HABIT

"It's important to turn disciplined behavior into a habit: early to bed, not too many splurges in my day-to-day routine. However, as a professional athlete it's really important not to fall prey to habit. Success on the court means being able to adapt to changing conditions, to different players, playing styles and more. One of the things I love most about tennis is that it's an ever-changing game. No two matches are alike, and the responsiveness to change is what sets great players apart. For me, a huge part of recuperating from my shoulder injuries was about being in touch with my body and every action's reaction. The ability to tune in and edit my response was the way I was able to unlearn the bad habits I'd fallen into from my injury. Being able not only to adapt but to anticipate the need to adapt is more important to me than habit."

Sharapova is a tennis player and memoirist.

THOMAS KELLER
ON HABIT

"I'm a naturally habitual person. I find that I'm comfortable in situations or environments where repetition is the norm, and I try to establish that wherever I go. In kitchens, we're all looking for greatness. And in order to be great, you have to be consistent. Do you want to be a Peyton Manning, a Derek Jeter? What makes these guys who have been in the game 20 years great is that they're great every day they go out and play. Does habit interfere with inspiration? Not at all. If I'm cleaning a salmon, in the first two years of doing that I'm really paying attention. But after a while, I don't have to concentrate so much. It becomes habitual, which allows me to start thinking about what I'll do with the salmon once I've cleaned it—look at the fat content of the belly or what to do with a fillet. That's when you can start to be inspired by the salmon. You become liberated by repetition."

Keller is a chef.

PALOMA PICASSO

ON HABIT

"I resist habit. One of the reasons I started traveling at an early age—on my own, and for work—is that travel has always been a way of stepping out of habit. If you're in a different place, you do things differently. When designing a collection, I often use high tables; but I've also worked while lying on the floor or sitting on a plane. I'm not a person who needs to design out of a special studio or with special tools. My father [Pablo] never had a special hour for working; there was nothing he did particularly geared toward habit. I created a perfume as a self-portrait that I wear almost every day. But the problem is that the smell becomes so much a part of you that you can't smell it any longer. So I have one or two other scents that I put on every now and then. When I break the habit, I can smell my fragrance again, which is really a part of me."

Picasso is a designer and businesswoman.

QUESTLOVE
ON INTUITION

"I'm a staunch supporter of rehearsing. I know to most people that seems like killing the spirit of intuition, killing the spirit of your first reaction. But I kind of live life coloring outside the lines, and coloring very meticulously inside the lines as well. The best improvisation happens when you've mastered whatever composition you're playing. So even if I'm in a situation when it's a jam session, when we're supposed to take the song where it wants to go, I believe you can only elevate an arrangement once you know it by heart. I prefer to practice my spontaneity. With intuition, I have a circle of five people who will actually say, 'You need to calm down a bit, you're overthinking.' That instinct has saved me. I'm smart enough to know that I will try to talk myself out of a good thing, so I have five friends whose job it is to talk me out of sabotaging myself."

Questlove is a record producer and drummer for The Roots.

IRIS
APFEL

ON COLOR

"I never met a color I didn't like. I
approach it the way I approach all
other things: totally unintellectual,
completely on gut feeling. I try to
approach things with a painterly eye
so that if I'm designing a room or
putting together an outfit, I think
about it as if it were a canvas and
needed just a little spot of red here or a
little black over there. My apartment is
a little bit on the wild side, done in
parrot colors: dark browns and bright
blues, greens and reds. I have friends
who love to come here but say that
when they go home to their apartment
done in beige or celadon, they find it
more peaceful. Strangely, these
vibrant colors are very peaceful to me.
If I had to live in a celadon or a beige
room, I would get very nervous. Color's
a great mood swinger. I think it's one
of the most sensual things in the
world. I just can't picture a world
without color. I don't think I could live
without it."

Apfel is a design consultant.

MAGGIE STEBER
ON FEAR

"In 1988, I was in Haiti photographing a priest who was critical of wealthy Haitians. When I got to the church everyone was being searched. Once we were inside, the doors were shut and chained. Just as the priest raised the host to be blessed, a gang of 40 men with machetes and machine guns burst through the doors. They started slicing people. Pews were flying through the air. They set the place on fire. I started taking pictures, but I knew I needed to get out. So I ran— right down the middle aisle and into the arms of a man with a machete. There was nothing in that man's eyes. I really thought I would die that day. But he lost his grip, and eventually some of us got away. A friend got me on the first flight out. When I returned to New York, I had to decide whether I would go back. I decided to return, because the greatest lesson I took from it was that this was the same terror that Haitians lived with daily."

Steber is a photographer.

OCTAVIA SPENCER

ON COURAGE

"I still have stage fright—anything having to do with live audiences is terrifying. I start sweating profusely, and my heart rate gets really, really elevated. People always ask me, 'Why were you so sweaty on the red carpet?' Because it terrifies me! But I just take a deep breath and say a prayer of thanks, because every day that you get to do what you love is a very blessed day, it's a gift. You take the first wobbly steps out and then you're fine, but I tell you, it's the exact same thing every time—the fear never goes away. But the thing is, if I go out way too confident, then I'm not tapped into what I'm really feeling, which means I'm not really present. You have to allow yourself to be present and confront your fears, and that's what courage is. You have to do the thing that terrifies you."

Spencer is an actor.

ESTHER PEREL

ON VULNERABILITY

"Vulnerability exists in technology, in the environment, in human beings. It's the state of being exposed, the possibility of being attacked or harmed either physically or emotionally. A system is vulnerable if it's left some hole that can be manipulated that could threaten its security. A human feels vulnerable when opening up because that exposure could lead to being harmed. When a couple comes to therapy, much of the work is about helping them open up to one another—exposing the part of themselves that they struggle with sometimes, the part they might not always like. I don't feel vulnerable when I open up the parts of me that I am certain about. Rather, I feel vulnerable exposing you to the uncertainty. But it's essential to our relational life, our relationship with ourselves and to others and the world."

Perel is a psychotherapist and author.

ALI MACGRAW

ON LOVE

"I've found that love resonates enormously differently with age. For many of us, the young version is just the tip of the iceberg. It's all wrapped up with heat and excitement, and enough trashy literature and TV to completely shortchange the bigger picture of what it means with time. The definition for me has become the ability to be nonjudgmentally, compassionately, forgivingly connected to others. It's like the great John Lennon song 'All You Need Is Love.' Damn right. To live in the possibility of behaving toward all living things with love is going to determine our survival as a planet. But let me be clear: The early version—the fall off a cliff, what is he thinking, when is he going to call feeling—is really fun. Some of us never let go of wanting a hit of that. Love is bigger than that, but it's not instead of that. And it's a piece without which life is a little grayer."

MacGraw is an actor.

YOTAM
OTTOLENGHI

ON DISCIPLINE

"I don't think discipline applies to one single school of cooking. I don't think molecular gastronomy requires more discipline than rustic French cooking or mama's cooking in a Greek village. It's the idea that you put yourself completely into the process of cooking and don't cut corners. For me that applies to every kind of cooking. It's all about being alert to what's going on in the pot or in the pan. It's about a state of mind. I know a lot of people have this romantic image of going to the market and rummaging through your spice cabinet, but actually I do a lot of groundwork before I go into the kitchen to try things out. You really need to sit and think if you're going to produce quality recipes every week. There's something about the physical work in the kitchen—there's a limit to how much you can do. Even in the busiest kitchen, there's always a point at the end of the day when you go home."

Ottolenghi is a London-based author and restaurant owner.

KARL LAGERFELD

ON DISCIPLINE

"Discipline? Oh, I have none. Do you ask yourself when you breathe, why and how are you taking a breath? No. For me, it's normal. For me, life is discipline. It's not intentional—it is the way I live. So in that way, I'm not disciplined at all. It's not something I have to fight for. I'm just pleased with what I'm doing, and I'm lucky to do it in great conditions and with people I like. I don't have to battle with anybody, and everybody does exactly what I want them to. Perhaps that is my suggestion: If you do something that you love, you won't need to force yourself to do it. Love and discipline: Are they that different?"

Lagerfeld is the creative director of Chanel and Fendi.

MELLODY
HOBSON

ON DISCIPLINE

"I'm hardwired to be disciplined.
I never needed an alarm clock as a
child. What you have to work against is
discipline to the point of being too
rigid. Rigid people are dangerous,
which becomes obvious when you look
at some of the financial firms that
went under. We're in the business of
numbers. The numbers have to be right
every time—there has to be zero-error
tolerance. I tell my team all the time,
'If you have a problem, the only way to
fix it is if you have a process you can
dissect, so that when something is
missed you can go back to your source
document.' I do better with order than
chaos, but at the same time I can be
very fluid. Discipline should be
balanced with flexibility. There are
people who are so disciplined that a
change upsets their constitution.
But survivors rescue themselves—they
never point fingers, or wait for
someone else to rescue them."

Hobson is the president of Ariel
Investments in Chicago.

HANS ZIMMER

ON LIMITS

"When I start a film score, the first thing I do is figure out what I'm not going to do. I set limits for myself. Is this going to be an orchestral score? Am I going to go to Africa and record a choir? I have so many choices available to me that if I don't limit the palette right from the beginning I'm never going to get anything done. A good film score needs to create a sonic world, and it needs to stay true to that world. *Dunkirk* is very specific in its sonic palette. The couple of times that it steps beyond the limits we set for ourselves, like when you hear a harmonious chord, come as a complete surprise. And the value of stepping outside those limits is much greater by having been disciplined up until that point. These limits force you to reinvent, they force you into being truly creative and having a point of view."

Zimmer is a composer.

DAVID
HALLBERG
ON LIMITS

"I've realized my limitations as a dancer, an artist and an athlete because I went beyond them. I experienced such heights, but I abused an instrument, and eventually, I crashed and burned because of my ankle injury. I lost all sense of hope that I would recover. But over time I learned to accept it, and consequently, I learned my limits. I learned when to say no. I learned that rest is just as important as work. At rock bottom, I reassessed my drive and reason for being. It's those kinds of limitations that save you. The experience has made me a better person. Now, having come out on the other side and performing onstage again, I'm certainly more humble. I also feel a sense of gratitude toward friends, lovers, toward my art form—that's true honesty. That's really what I've found."

Hallberg is an author and a principal dancer with the American Ballet Theatre.

LOUISE ERDRICH

ON LIMITS

"At first I thought, What limitations? Because I think of myself as somehow without them. It is absurd, but I do. A moment later, I realized I am defined by limitations. In fact, limitations are a positive force in my life. I need them. When I am stuck, I often write within a form, to a deadline, or otherwise set up fences around what I can do. Perhaps the imposition of rules spurs me to break free. Writing a novel is always about establishing and then pushing against parameters. For instance, when I was writing *The Round House*, which contains an unfolding crime mystery, I was using a first-person narrator. He was a young teenage boy. In order to move the story along he had to overhear or coax knowledge out of adults. This sort of tactic has to be used sparingly, so I tried to get him to discover clues from a multiplicity of places. That was wonderfully taxing, like playing a game with set rules, a challenging form of entertainment."

Erdrich is an author.

DAN SAVAGE

ON OPTIMISM

"I have a sort of photonegative, pessimistic take on optimism. I call it worst-case-scenario disorder. The only way to prevent bad things from happening is to anticipate them—I can only be optimistic after torturing myself with the worst possible outcomes. I can't get on a plane without picturing it crashing! A society can't flourish without optimism, because it's a form of cultural oxygen. But does it inoculate our society against collapse or nuclear war? No. So optimism has to be tempered by realism in order for it to be tolerable and workable. We've all met a Candide or Pollyanna—the 'God himself couldn't sink this ship' kind of optimists. That's annoying. Because, listen, the *Titanic* is at the bottom of the ocean. You have to be able to look at every ship and think, What can I do to make sure it doesn't sink? You can be optimistic about your efforts, but outcomes are never guaranteed."

Savage writes the column "Savage Love" and hosts the Savage Lovecast podcast.

KARLIE KLOSS

ON ESCAPE

"Escaping does not necessarily mean a break from reality. It's being present in reality. I've found a sense of escape through dance, or through something as simple as going for a run. I've also traveled the world to the most extraordinary, exotic places. And yet when I really want to find a sense of peace and happiness, I mentally escape to my grandmother's house in St. Louis. I spent a lot of time growing up there; it's preserved in my mind. I have these amazing memories. I can visualize every picture frame on every shelf, every pot and pan in the kitchen. On Saturday morning I'd wake up and smell the cinnamon toast that she made for us. I can see her in her slippers. For me, when I focus all my senses on escaping to that place in my memory, it's as powerful and calming as being by the ocean or a big body of water."

Kloss is a model and entrepreneur.

TAO LIN

ON STYLE

"The writing style I've always been attracted to is one that is working completely in service of the content. There are some books that are very stylized—prose poetry, something like James Joyce's *Finnegans Wake*—but often that style doesn't seem to actually be tied to the meaning of the work. With a writer like Hemingway, it seemed like he was just trying to be as concise and direct as possible, and that resulted in a distinct style. That approach seems necessary to me—I'm writing to convey meaning. Some have perceived an affectlessness in my work, but that's a side effect of my style, which can be very literal. In some novels I don't use any colloquialisms, so the characters almost sound like robots talking. I didn't want to include myself as an author, writing lyrical passages about death or something, so that was left out. But to me, the characters still feel emotions, so in that sense I don't view it as affectless."

Lin is a novelist, short story writer and poet.

ANNA DELLO RUSSO
ON STYLE

"Style is a communication of your personality. It doesn't matter what the type of style is, but it matters what you express. If you cannot express something, you do not have style. I like wild, violent style, so I don't like when it has too much direction by outside influences. The best style is when you are a teenager, when you're new and not too educated, before you've really entered society and the influence of the culture and the people around you. When I was a teenager, people made fun of me: Where are you going all dressed in yellow or pink or with that hat? My father used to say, 'Go ahead, don't care about other people.' Luckily I made fashion my job and finally I can dress however I wish. I loved the *Vogue* editor Diana Vreeland. Rather than teach fashion advice, she would always say, 'Why not?' For me, that's the right expression to educate people: Why not try? It's important not to be afraid, to be bold. Otherwise it's not style, it's a cage."

Dello Russo is the editor-at-large for Vogue Japan.

TARYN
SIMON

"My father obsessively documented his life. So from a very young age, I experienced a larger world through his Kodachrome slideshows, which detailed his travels to Afghanistan, Iran, Russia, Thailand and beyond. He was also a news junkie. So I was exposed to all the troubles of the world in vivid color from day one. But I was also pushed to look beyond the readily visible. Everything had an underbelly—governance, justice, even the East River. I remember the stories of pinball machines resting at the base of the East River. Mayor Fiorello La Guardia had rounded them up and smashed them with sledgehammers as a protest against the machines, which were being positioned as corrupting children. I guess I'm led by anxiety, fear and a want to see everything. The universe delivers a lot of unknowns. But humans crave certainty, no matter how falsely based."

Simon is an artist.

MARY LOU RETTON

ON COMPETITIVENESS

"I'm a coal-miner's daughter from a little town in West Virginia. I was the youngest of five children in a very loud, athletic family. People think gymnastics made me competitive, but it was really growing up in that dynamic. I was the pesky sister who always wanted to prove herself. Thirty-plus years ago, there weren't many opportunities for girls in sports. Still, I became a gymnast. Nobody had actually seen one like me. Back in my day, the stereotypical gymnast was tall and slender. I was told that I didn't have the right body. The media called me thunder thighs! But that worked for me. If you tell me I can't do something, I'll show you I can. Nowadays, I occasionally struggle with competitiveness. When I'm waiting in my car for the red light to change, I have to be the first one out of the gate. It's crazy! But I'm learning I don't have to be an Olympic champion every time."

Retton is a retired gymnast and an Olympic gold medalist.

URSULA BURNS

ON COMPETITIVENESS

"I'm a very competitive person. Competitiveness is absolutely necessary to be a great businessperson today. Everyone needs what I call a good enemy. From a business perspective, the good enemy is the competition in the marketplace. The good enemy forces you to excel. The good enemy is the benchmark, so you push yourself to be better. Competitive people want to be distinguished; they want to be associated with change. That said, it's definitely a behavior, along with assertiveness, that's adored and admired in men but considered inappropriate in women. The problem is that these behaviors negatively impact women more than things like compassion or a soft nature— attributes commonly associated with women—negatively impact men.
So women have to figure out a way to do the same thing without appearing to have the same behaviors as men."

Burns is chairman of Veon.

JANE KRAKOWSKI

ON WIT

"I remember being gifted a Dorothy Parker collection. I was so taken by her sharp wit. And then there are people like Tina Fey, another individual I'd call a true wit. I love the long-term collaboration I've had with her—two characters now. We've been able to do so much on *30 Rock* and on *Unbreakable Kimmy Schmidt*. I hope wit comes through in all the characters I portray. I find something funny when it lives on many levels— a level of self-deprecation, of knowl- edge and heightened reality. But it's very surprising to me to see how politically correct we've become. I wonder where we can go from here. I actually did a one-woman show based on it. Female movie stars from the pre-Code era of Hollywood, like Mae West, could be so raunchy and witty before they were edited. Sometimes they could go further in their wit than we go now."

Krakowski is an actor.

JOSÉ ANDRÉS

ON IMPULSE

"There are two types of impulses. Perhaps you see someone who is about to get hit by a car, and you have the impulse to save that person—anyone would agree that that's a good impulse. The 2016 presidential election is probably the perfect example of the other kind of impulse. The dictionary would describe it as the sudden, strong and unreflective desire to act or say something. In my case, I welcome impulsiveness in the kitchen and encourage it among my team. Impulse can be incredibly motivational.
You must give yourself the freedom to create and use those moments of creativity, those impulses, to move forward. Impulse could be described as jumping off a cliff. The most creative people, therefore, are those who are not afraid to throw themselves over a cliff, not knowing what's below."

Andrés is a chef and restaurateur.

JAMES HETFIELD

ON IMPULSE

"I have an addictive personality, so when I act impulsively it can go very wrong. In the band's early days, we didn't think at all—we lived in the moment. Usually that involved drinking or drugs or women. We destroyed our health on the road, until we realized that we couldn't play anymore, that I couldn't perform the way I wanted. The documentary *Some Kind of Monster* highlights the implosion of our band. We weren't caring for each other, because we didn't care enough about ourselves. It took all of that to make us realize we had a lot to be thankful for. I've learned that self-awareness is important, as is the ability to think impulsive ideas through to their natural conclusion. Now I'm spontaneous rather than impulsive, especially when I'm writing music or playing the guitar. I'm not planning any of that stuff. When I get a good guitar sound, it just happens—I'm only the messenger."

Hetfield is co-founder and lead vocalist of Metallica.

MINDY KALING

ON INNOVATION

"The hardest thing about comedy is when you can sense the effort, and you are repelled by it. When you have a group of comedy writers in a room, it's weird, because your job is to be funny, but it can't show too much effort. When we get to a funny area, we're talking about a heightened, documented conversation that we're having with our funniest friends. We have to shut off the parts of the brain that make it something we're stressed about, like work. It's all about observation and interactions, but I don't need to go to an art exhibit or Burning Man to get an idea. In fact, it's just the opposite. The more I run errands or do chores, the more inspiration I find. I get more out of filling my car with gas, getting it washed and returning some stuff to Best Buy than I would going to the library. So much of writing is repeating back into the script a funnier version of the thing you've just experienced."

Kaling is a writer and actor.

MARC MARON

ON ENVY

"I'm happy with my success, but I was certainly driven by envy and spite for most of my life. Validation is shifty in this business; if you're not capable of saying, 'I'm doing a good job,' how do you determine what it means to be successful? My envy and insecurity pushed other people away. I was preemptively defensive. Opportunities came to others, and I was resentful. I would call my manager and say, 'Why the hell is that guy getting that?' It eventually levels off, but not without a lot of wreckage and burned bridges. It took a lot to get out of that. The steps are: Acknowledge your limitations, accept what you do and then decide whether you're feeling healthy competitiveness or just beating yourself up. For some creative people who believe they are unique and underappreciated, it's a constant internal battle."

Maron is an actor, comedian and podcast host.

LORNA SIMPSON

"I've come to learn that hesitation is not necessarily procrastination but an opportunity to think about and expand upon an idea or project. Those who work creatively, like writers and musicians and artists, are constantly on deadline; there are demands from different places to finish and bring things right out into the world. But it's essential for us to protect and serve the creative process. I separate out the practicality of the management of the work and my studio from my relationship with the work. Certainly, I have to create space and a timeline to keep in mind, and sometimes I finish ahead of deadline, which is miraculous, but the creative process is the driving force. These demands are real, but I have to make the demands fit around my working process as an artist. Deadlines are important, but they should never disrupt or rule a trajectory of thought."

Simpson is an artist.

SEBASTIAN JUNGER

ON RISK

"I got out of risky reporting several years ago, but when I was working, the kind of risk I didn't like was when I had no control. You have a huge amount of control in combat—you can expose yourself or not, you're maneuvering on the ground, you can retreat. If you're in a situation where you're trusting people with guns to safeguard you, and suddenly they decide you look like a great hostage, you don't have control. Once you're in it, though, it becomes a random thing. During a firefight a bullet hit a few inches from my head. What's the gust of wind or the little angle that saved my life? Who knows. War reporting felt good because it felt meaningful, but I was at risk of repeating myself, which seemed like professional cowardice. And now I'm realizing other things are more meaningful. There's a point in your life when you start to live for others. Going to war hurts everyone who loves you. You're getting all the excitement. They just get the worry."

Junger is an author.

CHRISTIANE AMANPOUR
ON RISK

"As a war correspondent, there are inherent risks in what I do. I've always felt extremely responsible for my crew. And after I became a mother, my appreciation of my own personal risk changed exponentially. It was now my responsibility to stay alive for my son. But I also truly believe there is absolutely no substitute for firsthand field reporting—despite the advantages of the digital age. Without it, the world would not have known the real details about the genocides in Rwanda or Bosnia. Being an independent eyewitness is essential to reporting stories like the Arab Spring and the civil war in Syria. Being a foreign correspondent can be a risky profession, but if my son decides that he wants to be a journalist, I would love that. I believe this is a very noble profession. And because this job comes with great risk, you have to have passion and commitment."

Amanpour is a journalist, international correspondent and television host.

JAMES PATTERSON

"Some people believe that if something is very popular, it can't be very good. I don't agree. When something is popular I'm always curious about it. *Harry Potter* worked for me. *50 Shades* and *Twilight* didn't work so well. In general, the rule for success is *story, story, story*. When I write, I imagine one person sitting across from me. I'm telling a story, and I don't want them to get up until I finish. If I succeed, then I have a sense that I'll be popular. Ironically, my popularity actually makes me unpopular with some readers. And some of the books that I consider my best are my least popular. Part of it is that if I write something a little different, some fans go, 'Wait a minute, what is this? What is *The Jester*? This is back in the Crusades? Where's Alex Cross?' I'm not going to complain about not selling a lot of books, but that's one of the problems."

Patterson is an author.

JOHN PAWSON

ON PERFECTION

"I love perfect things. To me, it seems everything Mies van der Rohe did was perfect. The recognition of that quality is an emotional thing. When you walk in, you feel the light, the proportions and the materials working together to make a very special atmosphere. It's a visceral quality—hard to characterize, but absolutely unmistakable. Minimalism for me is really an attempt to get clarity. But it's a very fine line: Take away too much, and then you have nothing. If a building is clear, you have more natural light, but the flip side is that it exposes any sort of imperfections. At the beginning of a project for a new monastery we did in the Czech Republic, I remember saying to the monks that I wanted to try and get everything perfect. Normally if you speak to a client and say, 'I want to get it perfect,' they think that's marvelous. But the monks said that perfection is for God and not for man. Building isn't a precise business. It's human."

Pawson is a designer and architect.

MARY HELEN BOWERS

ON PERFECTION

"Ballet is all about the pursuit of perfection—it's the driving force behind the art. Dancers are famous for having incredible discipline, and if you're pursuing perfection it's going to take on an obsessive quality. You spend hours every day training, working on your body, and still, perfection is elusive. But too much perfection can be boring—it doesn't feel as soulful or as passionate. It can also be kind of cold. It's exciting when you watch a performer, and you're not sure what's going to happen. They have explosive energy when they're going for it; you think they're going to hit their turn, but you're not sure. I danced with the New York City Ballet, so I came up through the Balanchine system, where we were always taught it was better to try really hard. You might fall when you have that much energy, but it's exciting for the audience when you're giving it everything. To have a truly great performance, you have to be able to let yourself go on that level."

Bowers is the founder of the exercise program Ballet Beautiful.

LEE DANIELS

ON PERFECTION

"Perfectionists don't consider themselves perfectionists. We just strive to make things better—and they can always be better. It's kind of sad when you think about it. At the same time, I don't think you can embrace imperfection because then you're defeated. In my head, all of my characters are perfect. I have my idea of the story, and then there are the actors, with their interpretations. Later, you sit in the editing room, and it's like a piece of clay. You carve at it until you've cut it down to the essential elements of the story. Eventually, the producers say, 'OK, it's time to get out, we don't have any more money.' By the time I leave, I go, Wow, that's not what I thought it was going to be. It's beautiful, but it's not what was in my head. To know if I got it, I watch people react. If they're crying or laughing, if they are appalled, if I've hit the buttons of emotion in a deep way, then I know I've done my job."

Daniels is a producer and director.

NATHAN ENGLANDER

"I don't think fiction is an act of persuasion. Any intent like that corrupts the work. But a good book can absolutely change you. That's why it's a subversive form; that's why despots and totalitarians come after writers. But your intent shouldn't be to persuade. You can be passionate; you can even have a position. But the idea shouldn't be that you're trying to change someone's mind. The novels that saved me posed questions in a brutal manner, but they didn't give you the answers. I'd say that even about Orwell. He showed us the experiment of *Animal Farm*, but it's not didactic. The same is true of Kafka. As a writer, you're simply trying to share. It's about empathy. The mind is not changed or persuaded by fiction; it's literally altered. And that's different from my trying to get you to switch cable providers. Now *that's* persuasion."

Englander is an author.

AMY
SEDARIS
ON STYLE

"I don't think I have style. You know
those people who sell Christmas trees?
That's how I dress. I look like a beat-up
scarecrow. I'm like, oh well. People are
going to think I'm John Cougar
Mellencamp walking down the street.
I remember once I was going over to
Justin Theroux's house, and he said,
'Oh God, there might be paparazzi,'
and I was like, 'They'll just think I'm
Daniel Craig with a big coat on.' No
one's taking a picture of me. I like
performance wear, clothing where it
feels like one size fits all, with a good
sturdy zipper. Then when I have to go
out and dress up, I feel special. I like it
when kind of unattractive people go
out of their way to look attractive. I
love that. Jerri Blank, the character I
played on the show *Strangers with
Candy*, had the hair of a professional
golfer, an overbite, nicotine-stained
teeth and below her waist was a
problem area. But she had big fancy
eyelashes and accessorized with
pizzazz, so I think she had great style."

Sedaris is an actor, comedian and writer.

ADAM PHILLIPS
ON POSSESSION

"Possession has in it the idea of avoiding loss. If you own a lot of things, you're less vulnerable to loss. It's very likely that in this culture the idea of an enviable life has replaced the idea of a good life. If I'm somebody who possesses a great deal of desirable objects then I'm both immune to loss and I'm an object of envy and admiration. And that could sustain a picture of myself as leading the best life available to me, as though the best person is the richest person. On the one hand you want to possess something so you no longer need to go on wanting it—the question of possession begins very early on, and it's about acquiring a sense that the wish to possess is a magical solution to the problem of frustration. But the issue is, if you possess something before you really want it, you won't know what to do with it when you get it."

Phillips is a psychotherapist and author.

PAT CLEVELAND
ON POSSESSION

"I was raised by my mother, and she bought *everything*. We used to go to Bloomingdale's and buy the most expensive items. She would buy a diamond even if we had to eat beans for weeks. When I was 15, she bought me a fur coat. She said, 'If you have this, it will open doors for you.' For my mother, living well was the best revenge. Her mother, my grandmother, was very well educated—she attended Spelman College—but had no opportunities. You see, she grew up in the deep South. Imagine going from picking cotton to Spelman. So possessions were not superficial things for my mother. They were meaningful. They meant that you had reached a certain point, that you *could* have the dream. And a thing becomes your companion. Your possessions tell your story."

Cleveland is a model and author.

JAY LENO

ON POSSESSION

"I have 150 cars and 117 motorcycles. But I don't buy cars to look at—mine are all functioning. A lot of times, you buy the story as much as you buy the car. A few years ago, I got a call from this 91-year-old woman. She had a 1951 Hudson Hornet. She had bought the car new with her husband. He died in '96, and since then it had been parked in the garage. She would go out with this big feather duster and wipe it off. It was in rough shape, but she was such a nice lady, I bought it and took it back to my garage to restore it. Two years later, I call her up and ask her to take a ride in this car. She says, 'Let me call the kids.' They're like 70 and 72! We get in the car and go for a ride. She's laughing and telling stories about the car and her husband, driving it from New Jersey to California in 1951. The kids are laughing. I'm saying, 'Stop it or I'm going to turn this car around.' We were hysterical. It was so much fun."

Leno is a comedian, actor, philanthropist and television host.

DANIEL BOULUD

ON OBSESSION

"By nature, chefs are already pretty obsessed people. It takes a lot of perseverance and stamina to be able to become a great chef. If you want to be an Olympic swimmer or champion, you have to obsess about training for something like eight hours a day. Cooking is usually 12 hours a day. Everyone I know who is a chef like me has a devouring passion about being truly creative and attending to perfection all the time. We are fanatic about cleanliness, order, avoiding waste. I can see 20, 40 feet away something wrong in the dining room that no one else has seen: a napkin on the floor or a frame that's a little sideways. We always try to enforce a certain order of functioning, and it quickly becomes an obsession to maintain that. Your ambition drives your obsession and your obsession drives your ambition. I don't know which comes first."

Boulud is a chef and restaurateur.

ANNE BASS

ON TASTE

"Talking about taste is rather outdated, in a way. The former absolutes of taste no longer seem relevant. It's more about curation today, the development of personal preferences. The biggest influence on my taste was my grandmother. She was very quiet, very self-aware—there was never a big statement about what she was doing. She just knew how to create these environments, and it was always such a pleasure to be at her house. I think I've tried to re-create that feeling. And then my parents were constantly saying that restraint was desirable and that ostentation was not, and there was a lot of shoulds and should nots and notions of absolute taste, which I think may have propelled me toward a preference for orderly spaces. When it comes to gardens I love the combination of structure and freedom. I like it to feel very natural even though it's shaped. It should feel inevitable."

Bass is a philanthropist and documentary filmmaker.

CHARLES MASSON

ON MANNERS

"When I was a child, my parents used to take me out to a restaurant once a week, even though they didn't necessarily have the means. Restaurants are a wonderful space for a child to learn the value of good behavior because, in dining, the rules of etiquette are built on respect. But the trouble with rules is that once you establish them you may find yourself bending to the breaking point. If someone is speaking loudly on their cellphone and there are other guests trying to have quiet conversation, you might approach the guest and ask them to take the call outside. But you have to be casual, because if you enact a policy that forbids cellphone use in this day and age, your restaurant will be empty. It's also bad form to make a reservation for six and arrive alone without calling in advance. In those situations, you don't say anything to the guest; you just remember!"

Masson is a restaurateur.

LYNN WYATT

ON MANNERS

"My husband and I have four sons and two grown grandchildren. Good manners were as important to their education as their schooling. When our grandchildren came to our house, their parents would say, 'Mind your Mimi's manners!' It's all about treating people with courtesy and kindness. For instance, it's impolite to call someone after 10 in the evening unless it's an emergency. And I think it's always best to converse with someone in person, eyeball to eyeball, when possible— the inflection of someone's voice is missing in an email, and a text message can be very misleading. If ever I'm asked an ill-mannered question, I just say, 'I'll forgive you for asking me that question if you'll forgive me for not answering it.' Oh, and the absolute worst thing is spitting! To have good manners means simply to be considerate of others—it's what allows us to all get along."

Wyatt is a philanthropist and socialite.

JOSHUA FOER

ON MEMORY

"At the bottom of all the ancient memory techniques is the notion of forced attention. I think it was Samuel Johnson who said the true art of memory is the art of attention. A lot of memory techniques are ultimately about transforming information into the kind of information that your brain naturally pays attention to. I think that's something you can will into existence. We all know the experience of sitting in a boring talk and kind of dozing off and saying to ourselves, Okay, snap back into this, don't fall asleep. That's something that you can do in your life if you keep the importance of that at the front of your mind. It's a kind of mindfulness. In the case of memory competitions, you're applying it to these really circumscribed, discrete tasks, but the general principle can be broadened to the rest of your life, to make sure that you're not zipping through it all with your eyes closed."

Foer is an author.

KRISTIN SCOTT THOMAS

ON LIMITS

"The word *limit* does have an image of barrier, an image of something that should not be crossed. But as an actor you are required to push against your limits, even though a lot of people do not want you to go beyond your perceived boundaries—rather, they want you to repeat the thing they know you're successful at. How I manage to satisfy my curiosity and all other feelings of being calcified in some roles is by taking on theater. I played Sophocles's Electra in London [in 2014]. It was quite risky for me to take on the part, because traditionally she's played as a very young woman and I was middle-aged. I did go as far as I was able to in that role. My God, it was exhausting, but it was definitely worth it. It moved 16-year-old girls.
It raised questions about mothers and daughters, about daughters and fathers. Being able to push against these perceived limits is what makes life interesting."

Thomas is an actor.

LUCY
LIU

ON ESCAPE

"In acting, you're not just escaping your mind; to completely embody a character, you have to go to a soul level. The ability to spend some time in that space is incredibly freeing. You are constantly searching, changing things. It's a sort of playground, and it should be playful and fun even if it's a dark character, because you can get outside of yourself. Which doesn't happen often. Most people are like, 'You're not yourself!' It's usually a negative comment. But in this case, you don't want to be yourself—not being yourself is a compliment. When you're acting and you're really immersed in it, you don't even know what happened in the last two minutes. When you're so connected to something that you're taken completely out of your world, out of your body, time is condensed and almost disappears. That's when you really allow and invite another part of yourself to come in."

Liu is an actor.

RAINN WILSON

ON PROGRESS

"Gasoline used to make this big knocking sound, so they added lead to it. That eliminated the sound in engines, but eventually they realized this lead was coming out of the exhaust and entering the atmosphere. They literally found lead in the snow in Antarctica. It was like this giant step backward. You have to remember that just because you move something forward doesn't mean it's progress. It's an argument that has been going on since the dawn of time—what is progress and what is not? What Aristotle thought was progress, what Plato and Socrates thought was progress, was greatly debated. We're a culture that doesn't believe in moderation. I'm in that stage of parenting right now where some of those very simple adages really do hold true. 'Day by day, little by little.' That's how progress works."

Wilson is an actor and memoirist.

LAURIE
METCALF
ON EXPECTATIONS

"When I first started out I never
expected to make a living from
acting—I was too practical—so I
always had a backup secretarial job.
I never expected to be able to build a
career from something that I
otherwise would have done for free. I
would have just acted in community
theater, for the hell of it, because I feel
most creative and happy and alive
when I'm performing. I understood
that the odds were stacked against me.
I would have to be the proverbial
needle in the haystack in order to go
from a tiny town in Illinois and end up
performing in New York or Los Angeles
or London, and I didn't want to set
myself up for failure. It's scary to go
out on a limb. I was an original
member of Steppenwolf Theatre
Company, and frankly, if it weren't for
that group I would have chickened out.
I wouldn't have trusted I could make it
on my own."

Metcalf is an actor.

ANNE
APPLEBAUM
ON EXPECTATIONS

"As a historian, you're often at war
with clichés, which are something
similar to expectations. People have
stereotyped images of the past; I seek
to make them more complicated.
In that sense, any good history book
defeats expectations because it offers
a richer tapestry, a more complicated
version of what most people think
happened. History can also alter how
we think about the future. Although
history does not provide a road map of
what to expect in the future, it does
tell you what kinds of situations should
cause concern. Human emotions don't
really change that much. The study of
history can tell us how people once
reacted to certain kinds of events, and
can therefore help us know what to
expect. The present is not the 1930s,
for example—but if you read about it,
you will find elements of the 1930s
that have an echo in the present, which
should both interest and worry you."

Applebaum is an author.

WANGECHI MUTU

ON EXPECTATIONS

"I don't know what audiences expect from my art. Maybe I resist actually thinking about that, because you don't want to be entertaining people. Rather, you want to be thinking about things in depth. I try not to worry too much about the applause, if there is any or ever will be. When I first started my professional practice, I was completely alone in my studio. Not many people knew who I was. But as my career picked up it became more obvious to me that there is commentary and expectation, even as I'm tucked away at work in my studio. Outside elements seep in, because you can't ignore the fact that the world is aware. The gift for me has always been finding the sweet spot where the silence is real. It protects you from your inability to be free and open. I really worked to get to that point."

Mutu is an artist.

TODD HAYNES

ON EXPECTATIONS

"Filmmaking is about letting expectations go at every step of the way. Hitchcock claimed to have constructed all of his films in storyboards, but his best movies work because he used steps later in the filmmaking process— shooting, editing, scoring—to build on his original idea. In filmmaking, you can't keep looking back at how you envisioned a story on the page. I've only recently undertaken adaptations from novels, from *Mildred Pierce* to *Carol* and now *Wonderstruck*, and I don't put a lot of energy into navigating readers' prior expectations. Because, ultimately, the real question is, Why is this a movie at all? There are plenty of great books, famous lives and subjects out there that don't necessarily have to be made into movies. There needs to be a good reason *why*."

Haynes is a film director.

JANE GOODALL

ON CURIOSITY

"I was totally curious as a child. I once took worms to bed, wondering how they walked without legs. I watched intently as they moved about. Chimpanzees are very curious too. If they come across a hole in a tree, they want to know what's inside. Curiosity is supposed to be a measure of intelligence, but it's difficult to say. Intelligence is the way you express curiosity and the lengths you'll go to satisfy it. We're always coming up with new questions. Science thinks it's got the answer to the appearance of the universe with the big bang, but that leads me to ask, 'What came before the big bang?' I still have a lot of questions. What will happen to me as I get older? What will happen to me when I die? That's my biggest curiosity and has been for a long time. But you can't find an answer. It's unknowable."

Goodall is an ethologist and anthropologist.

SIMON DE PURY

ON ENVY

"In art collection, there are as many different motivations as there are different collectors. In some cases, envy may play a role. But I think perhaps it's more about emulation— collectors trying to emulate what another has done. When I see a truly great collection, I am in awe, because I consider collecting an artistic pursuit in its own right. So a great collector to me is like an outstanding artist. Take collectors like Leonard Lauder or Peter Brant—it's sheer pleasure to see what one individual has been able to acquire. I can't even begin to see why one should feel envious of it. The best way to make yourself miserable is to be envious. In art auctions, competition plays a much bigger role than envy, as collectors compete to find the best works. The desire to excel at something, that competitive streak, is absolutely healthy. But envy will never make you happy."

De Pury is an auctioneer and art dealer.

PETER SINGER

ON ENVY

"The classic expression of envy is in Tom Wolfe's novel *The Bonfire of the Vanities,* where the guy who makes a million dollars a year working on Wall Street is envious of someone who has a permanent limo driver. Once you have that attitude, you can never have enough. I'm sure there are circumstances where envy can lead to something positive, where because someone is envious of the success of others, they work harder and are able to achieve things that may benefit everyone. But that can also happen without envy. I really believe that giving significant sums to charities helps quell envy because you get more satisfaction out of giving money away than spending it on yourself. You cease to be envious of others who have more—why do you need to buy an expensive watch or car when there are much more worthwhile things to do with your money?"

Singer is an author and professor of bioethics at Princeton University.

RICKY GERVAIS

ON PATIENCE

"I'm the least patient person I know. I suppose if you're talking about the bigger picture, nurturing something like my work on a script, then I do have patience in the long term, but day-to-day, no. If I walk into a shop, and there's a queue of one person, I'll come back. Life's too short. I'm not impatient that a tree's not growing fast enough, but if I want to plant a tree, then that shop needs to be open to sell me that acorn right now. And I'm always early. If I'm meeting someone, whether it's an important meeting or just something social, I'm 15 minutes early. So if they're one minute late, they are 16 minutes late in terms of how annoyed I am. I don't know an excuse good enough not to be on time. Death is the only thing that gets someone back into my good books for being late. Where is he? He's dead? He's definitely dead? Okay . . . fine."

Gervais is a comedian, writer, producer and actor.

ANNA KENDRICK

ON PROCRASTINATION

"I'm not the type of person who does things on time. I feel as though if I'm going to answer one email, I should also open every other piece of mail, I should call my mom and dad and brother. All those things the perfect version of you would do, but she never comes! Setting out to write a memoir was like someone saying, 'Build your own house from scratch.' At first I thought that I might magically become one of those people who wrote on weekends or for an hour every night. But I am so not one of those people. When I finally came up against my third deadline, I decided to lock myself in a room for five days and be unbelievably strict with myself. Soon the task started to feel less insurmountable. Not all of it ended up in the final book, but at least I had written something— even if it wasn't immediately obvious, there was value in doing it."

Kendrick is an actor.

ALAN MENKEN

ON PROCRASTINATION

"In the '70s there was this motivational program called EST. You trained yourself to avoid procrastination because, as you learned, it was not only counterproductive, it also caused you pain. As a composer, I find that collaboration is a huge boon to overcoming procrastination since there's always someone depending on you. I don't like to disappoint people, so the last thing I'm going to do is procrastinate. Often, I'll make an appointment with my collaborator, and I don't leave the studio without having made some progress. But then there's the benign version of procrastination: patience. The further you get in your career, the more you begin to recognize that there is power and benefit in letting your thoughts marinate. Sometimes it's OK to wait, to walk away for a bit."

Menken is a composer.

MELISSA ARNOT REID

ON PROCRASTINATION

"Procrastination is a trap to which we're all susceptible. Fear is often the silent driver of our actions—we fear failure and success equally. I'm driven once I choose to do something, but the decision to do it is where I really exercise procrastination. Sometimes when you're making a difficult climb, the longer you hesitate to move, the more fatigued you get. That's kind of a brilliant metaphor for life: The more you stand in procrastination, the less of an ability you have to leap to the next step. You do a lot of groundwork to prepare for a climb and then you have this choice, this moment when your actions will dictate your success or failure relative to getting to the summit or your safety. It's easy then to feel intense pressure knowing that these kinds of decisions are the turning point of all the work that you've done; the outcome is so unknown. But you have to move."

Arnot Reid is a mountain climber and adventurer.

ALBER ELBAZ

ON LUCK

"I was born in Morocco, and our culture is all about this kind of stuff—you are lucky, you are unlucky, you are in the right place or not. Now mix it with intuition, with sensitivity, with imagination. Can you push the luck, or is it destiny? It's all very abstract. Luck can bring you to the door. Now what do you do in the room? This is up to you. I don't think there are people who are lucky and those who are not. Still, I am a very superstitious man—I don't talk about my collections. I also don't think luck is something you can control. I think the thing that makes people different is whether or not you grow with love. If you can grow with love around you, from your surroundings, your family, your friends, you are lucky—when you don't grow with love, you are unlucky. This is what I define as luck. Both luck and love start with an L."

Elbaz is a fashion designer.

BENJAMIN CLEMENTINE
ON STATUS QUO

"It's important for all of us to tap into things that make us uncomfortable. It's good to challenge yourself as an artist, because that opens portals to new discoveries. I'm always looking for ways to tap into my vulnerability, to provoke something I never knew before. The people I adore, from Tom Waits to Prince to Virginia Woolf, they changed things. Look at David Bowie. Look at Jimi Hendrix. They experimented. I can never be like them; I can only hope that one day I will have my own sort of space. It's not that I want people to think I'm different for superficial reasons. It's merely about expressing things your own way. And if you do what you want to do and it's similar to someone else, that's fine, too. But it's quite fulfilling to be able to do things your way. I suppose that's what being an artist is really all about."

Clementine is a singer-songwriter.

JOHN LITHGOW

ON STATUS QUO

"To me the status quo is, as the Latin says, the present moment, the way things are now. But I guess the larger meaning of it is somewhat like the word *zeitgeist*—what is the prevailing mood? The movie industry is odd, because on the one hand it has to reinforce people's prejudices so as to appeal to what they want to see—it resorts to clichés in a sense—but on the other hand it's an industry that can change people's minds. Take movies like *Moonlight*, for example, or *Easy Rider*. They're little films that turn into big revolutionary statements. In *Beatriz at Dinner*, I play a billionaire real estate developer, an archetype for our times. It's a movie about a dinner party where all the standard procedures are disrupted. It becomes a really interesting metaphor because, boy, are we at a moment when standards are being disrupted. What's going to happen when we don't have any structures to fall back on?"

Lithgow is an actor.

CARRIE FISHER

ON CONFIDENCE

"Confidence is a bad thing to have as a drug addict. No drug addict deserves confidence. For me, taking drugs had to do with blurring sharp feelings and turning off the extraneous areas of my mind that wanted to talk to me about stuff from my past. It was a nice way to turn it off. I was playing a person called Carrie Fisher and I was trying to get out of character. That was drug taking for me. Now I'm confident enough to stay in my mind without drugs. Though, weirdly, some of that was taught to me by taking LSD. You had to be confident that you could end up anywhere in your brain, even parts that could harm you. You had to learn to trust the instrument and feel that you had nothing to hide. But if you're taking drugs for your emotions, to diminish them, then you should not have confidence. You should be very afraid."

Fisher was an actor and writer.

JOE GEBBIA

"The fear of mistakes is the fast track to irrelevance. Of course Airbnb made mistakes the first year! Some came from our own preconceptions. When we started, we designed our interface for ourselves, internet-savvy twenty-somethings. We never considered the role of good eyesight in our interface—font size, vernacular; it all matters. The fastest-growing group of Airbnb hosts in the United States is seniors; the second-fastest-growing group is people in their 50s. So we learned our lesson. On a recent Mother's Day we invited our moms to visit the company, and we encouraged them to use the website in front of us. We were able to witness firsthand if something didn't work for them. But it's important to remember that the failure itself is not an event. It's the relationship that you choose to have with an event—how you react to it—that matters."

Gebbia is cofounder and chief product officer of Airbnb.

ANDY COHEN

ON CHARM

"I know a lot of charming people, and
when I think of charm, I think of a
smile that's very disarming and
inviting. You might turn on the charm
in an effort to seduce someone else,
and I don't necessarily even mean a
sexual seduction—although, listen,
Julia Roberts in *Pretty Woman* really
knew how to turn on the charm—
it's just simply about trying to get
someone into your favor. When I'm on
tour with Anderson Cooper, we want to
charm our audience so they feel good
about spending money on a ticket. It's
also important for me to attempt to be
charming every night on my show,
even when I'm not feeling so charming.
The other night, for example, I
received very bad news about an old
friend. But it's not about what you're
going through; it's about being the
best and most charming version
of yourself."

*Cohen is a talk show host, producer
and author.*

ALEXANDRA FULLER

ON CHARM

"I was raised with a very colonial,
shallow understanding of charm, this
fragile set of rules that usually
emphasized language. My mother
might remark that someone had
charming manners, but what she really
meant was that they knew the rules to
get into 'the club.' The irony is that I
was surrounded by violence, lots of
neglect, bouts of alcoholism—just
really bad behavior—yet as long as you
knew never to say to someone, 'Would
you like another drink?' but rather
'How about the other half?' my mother
would approve of your charming
manners. Real charm is about authenticity. The most charming people have
knowledge of self through cultural and
spiritual integrity. I'm at my most
charming when I'm not taking myself
too seriously, and that's hard to do
because it requires relinquishing one's
bloody ego. Charm doesn't alter; it
doesn't break under pressure."

Fuller is a writer.

SAM ELLIOTT
ON CHARM

"Like most words in any language, the word *charm* has two faces. On one side you have those really delightful people, the ones we all love to be around. But on the flip side there is a kind of charm that is less sincere, that's used to manipulate others. Anyone who uses charm for personal gain is not particularly nice, and in the end that's really what it's about—treating people the way you want to be treated. I worked briefly with Jimmy Stewart on one job, and he was just the nicest man. He was exactly that character I'd seen in so many of his films, that lovable, charming human being. He was a great actor, although he wasn't a chameleon. Gary Cooper was another charming person. The guys from those days were just really good at being themselves. Now, that's charm."

Elliott is an actor.

TIG NOTARO
ON CHARM

"For the most part, I always feel very much like myself, but at times I can definitely sense a slight shift in my personality, like when I'm around a stranger. I'm probably most charming onstage. I want the audience to like me. I want to get the right response from them, and that's obviously laughter. In the writer's room for my show, *One Mississippi*, I made a very clear point to the other writers that I didn't want to be a flawless character, because that would be boring. I think flawed characters—the ones you see struggling in an authentic way to change and grow—are the funniest and most charming. It's like seeing a three-legged dog. So many of the characters on *One Mississippi* are three-legged dogs running around just trying to move through life with whatever's missing. There's nothing more touching, likable and charming than that."

Notaro is a comedian.

MARIE KONDO

ON WILLPOWER

"With willpower, I think about the balancing point between having the determination to start something and having the wisdom to stop. When I was younger I would reach a point in my tidying where I would throw out almost anything. My brother's stuff, my sister's—even my parents' and my teachers' things weren't safe. What for many people is so difficult to start— tidying—was sometimes difficult for me to stop. One of the most common questions I hear is, 'Your book helped me, but what can I do about the messiness of my husband, wife, co-worker, etc.?' I always answer the same way: 'Nothing. You can't change them, and you shouldn't try.' Show them what you have achieved through your tidy room, your freer soul, and let them find their own way forward. Willpower is not only the drive to change yourself, it's also the sense of understanding that this power has limits."

Kondo is an organization expert and author.

COMMON
ON LOYALTY

"In the inner city, loyalty is a way of life. It's something that people expect—it's a moral code—and hip-hop is a way of expressing those values. It was really pronounced in the era of Tupac and Biggie. Whether it was a coast or a crew, you announced your loyalty to the world through your music. That kind of loyalty is usually born out of shared experiences, something that leads to a bond between two people. I remember visiting my cousin in Cincinnati when I was a kid. One day, his friend— someone he knew from the block— and I got into an argument over basketball, so we decided that we were going to fight. We walked down to the corner and went at it. But soon it was clear I was getting beat up! So my cousin jumped in and, you know, he settled the argument. It really touched me. In that moment, his allegiance to me mattered more to him than anything else."

Common is a musician, actor, poet and film producer.

ABBY WAMBACH

ON TIMING

"The thing about timing in soccer is that you have to anticipate and guess what your teammate is about to do. Unlike other sports where there are set plays, soccer is free-flowing. That's why timing is one of the most important immeasurable intangibles, as we call them. When to move my body, when to jump for a header, where to anticipate the ball falling—there are so many variables. And every moment changes. What I focus on is putting my body in a position to force the ball into the goal. Instinct takes over: The ball is going to reach a certain point, and I need to get to that point at the perfect time, traveling at the perfect speed, so that it hits the perfect part of my head to go toward the goal. The reality comes down to time spent on the field with my teammates, to get that consistency. There's no such thing as a perfect play."

Wambach is a soccer player and an Olympic gold medalist.

ERIC RIPERT

ON TIMING

"It's mostly a sixth sense that tells me when a dish is done. One fish may take eight minutes to cook, another only three. A fish can be perfect right now and five seconds later it's overcooked. It goes that quickly. A soufflé stays up for like 10 seconds. It's the eyes, mostly, just looking at it. I may be distracted and busy doing something else, but it's rare that I forget to double-check. I always come back on time. I'm like that in my life, too, extremely punctual. Sometimes you can have a sense of timing about destiny. The minute I walked in on my first day at Le Bernardin, my sixth sense told me something special was happening. It was a June morning, 7:40 a.m.; I looked at my watch. I turned to my friend Scott, the sous chef, who was walking in with me, and I told him, 'Look at the time. This is important.' I'll always remember that moment."

Ripert is chef.

LINDSEY ADELMAN
ON POPULARITY

"Sometimes, as a designer, you can feel when you strike a nerve. When I started developing the Branching Collection in 2005, I had an inkling pretty early on that the pieces were going to connect with people. They became really popular. I had the intention of making a successful line in part because I wanted to be fiercely independent; I wanted to be my own boss. But I think it can be perceived that *I* wanted to be popular. I'm still not like that. Sometimes I design with the intention of reaching a wide audience. And then other times I design to express something, and that expression can be murky or dark or polarizing, but I just know it's important for me to make it. The most important thing I can do is to make work that's authentic and reflects where I am now. Beyond that I don't feel obliged to put out any kind of one-hit wonders, because that is death to me."

Adelman is a designer.

ELIZABETH GILBERT

ON EPIPHANIES

"Listen, I'm a memoirist. Anyone with 10 bucks can buy a copy of *Eat, Pray, Love* and read all about my epiphanies. The reason epiphanies feel so surprising is twofold. First, it's the surprise of seeing a truth revealed. Second, it's the deep shock of wondering why it took you so long to see it in the first place. It's something that was there all the while. Sometimes an epiphany can be very beautiful, like when you realize you're in love with your best friend. Other times it can be incredibly painful. For me, the biggest and most important personal epiphany of my life was that bouncing from man to man was not actually a path to happiness and fulfillment. The emptiness I was trying to fill was not going to be filled by leaping into the arms and bed of somebody else. But an epiphany is not an obligation. It's an invitation. What you do with that invitation is up to you."

Gilbert is an author.

KIM GORDON
ON POWER

"There are ways to create power onstage: Multiple guitars give a sense of power, especially with the bass coming underneath. There's a part in the [Sonic Youth] song 'Shaking Hell' when all the guitars were doing one thing and then the bass dropped down, and it kind of pushed it to another level. With unfriendly audiences, mostly we just ignored them. I didn't need to see them giving me the finger again. In fact, it can be powerful to make yourself vulnerable onstage. People respond to that. Having the audience responding to you, even just quietly listening—that's a powerful feeling. But I also think about the song 'Out of My Mind' by Buffalo Springfield. It's about finding yourself in the world of being a rock star, sitting in the back of a limo. You think you're supposed to feel powerful, but you just feel alienated. It's about how power is not what you think—you feel very alone."

Gordon is one of the founding members of the band Sonic Youth.

RYAN SEACREST
ON POWER

"As a broadcaster I have interviewed powerful people. My mentor, Dick Clark, told me to learn something from everyone I spoke to, and so I would listen and would think, and time after time I would come to the same conclusion: They were powerful because of their capacity to change lives for the better. Over the years, I'd been to children's hospitals and visited with patients and their parents and had spent moments with them, laughed with them and always wished there was more I could leave behind, which eventually led to creating a foundation with my parents and sister. All I know about power comes from those children, who fight every day, and from those parents, who need to know their boys and girls are OK, and that together they have a chance. In short, what I know about power is it comes from one place: giving."

Seacrest is a television and radio host and a producer.

KEVIN DURANT

ON POWER

"Something that's often overlooked in basketball is mental power. A game is 50 percent mental—mental toughness. Going through ups and downs during a long season, you have to really set your mind to have the power over everybody else—over opponents, fans, bad refs, tough games. You gotta fight through that. When I was young, I was always the skinny kid and got pushed around a lot, and my mental toughness goes back to that. There are so many strong and athletic guys in this league, and at the end of the day, there will always be someone taller, someone stronger, somebody quicker. Having that willpower and extra fight is what's going to set you apart. On the court there's trash talk, you can hear fans trying to disrespect you, but just being quiet, never being too high or too low, is the most powerful place to be in a game."

Durant is an NBA basketball player.

KELLY
WEARSTLER
ON COLOR

"Color is everything—it's more powerful than geometry, it just depends on how you use it. It's the first thing I start with when I'm working on my fashion collections or interior projects. When I'm designing a room, I always look at the adjacent rooms, or what's outside the window. I recently did a New York townhouse, and there was a brick red building visible through the windows. I chose a beautiful steel blue for the room, and the red gave it so much depth. Texture is also very important. A matte format or a lacquered format makes color read very differently. And people forget that white is a color: Ten different shades of white can make an impact as strong as malachite green. Sometimes clients tell me, 'I'm afraid of color but I like it.' I tell them to look at what's inside their closet. There will usually be one color they feel good in, which means that they will look good in a room of that color. Color makes people happy. Living without color is like living without love."

Wearstler is a fashion and interior designer.

RAY
KURZWEIL
ON THE FUTURE

"The reason we have a brain is to predict the future—so we can anticipate the consequences of actions and the consequences of inaction. That became good for survival and hard-wired into our brains. The common wisdom is that you cannot really predict the future. It's true for a lot of things but not about the capacity of information technology. I wrote an essay reviewing all of my predictions, including 147 I made about the year 2009. They were 86 percent correct. I started making these predictions more than 30 years ago. That's the power of exponential growth.

I'm optimistic about the future because it's different from what we see in science fiction films, where one evil individual gets ahold of a futuristic technology and threatens humanity. Artificial intelligence, in the form of devices like smartphones, is not in one person's hands—it's in one to two billion hands."

Kurzweil is an inventor, futurist and author.

HIROSHI ISHIGURO

ON PROGRESS

"I wasn't always interested in androids. I wanted to be an oil painter. I wanted to be an artist. But I went into science, and I found that robotics is quite an artistic job. Robots are my canvas. In building them, I'm trying to learn more about humankind. You see, technology is a kind of mirror. What are we? Why are we here? Of course, there will always be resistance. There will always be individuals who struggle to accept certain advancements, individuals who don't want to change their lifestyle and take longer to adapt to newer technologies. The Japanese have reacted more positively overall to my project because we don't really distinguish between humans and others—we believe everything has a soul. In the future, I think we'll have more humanlike robots. We already have an android talk-show host here. And after all, androids never complain!"

Ishiguro is director of the Intelligent Robotics Laboratory at Osaka University, in Japan.

JONATHAN FRANZEN

"Fiction is a sloppy form—perfection is beyond us. For Karl Kraus, the Viennese author I write about in my book *The Kraus Project*, perfectionism was related to notions of moral purity. He had mystical ideas about language, a spiritual feel for its primacy. When he says that being a writer means spending all morning deciding to take out a comma, and then going back after lunch and putting it back, I certainly know that side of it. But I don't think a novelist can afford to be wound so tightly. Paula Fox's *Desperate Characters* is as close to perfect as you can come, and I would argue that it's aware of this and kind of blows itself up at the end because it's so sick of trying to be perfect. Part of the near perfection of *The Great Gatsby* is that it feels relaxed and almost tossed off. Fitzgerald had a great ear, he heard the way people spoke, and he knew when to not overdo it. My own ear for overwriting has to do with my phobia of it. At this point, I would rather underwrite."

Franzen is an author.

JAY
MCINERNEY
ON INDULGENCE

"The interesting thing about indulgences is that they ultimately become flabby without a certain degree of abnegation. I quit drinking for the month of August, traditionally a month of fairly solid indulgence. It really heightened my appreciation: I enjoyed that first glass of wine in September about as much as I can ever remember appreciating a glass of wine. As someone who's been raised a devout Catholic, I find the shadow of guilt always adds piquancy to any indulgence. It's almost more pleasurable, feeling slightly guilty. William Blake famously said the road of excess leads to the palace of wisdom, but I think it's more likely that creative people tend to have excessive personalities, rather than that excessive behavior being a useful aid to creativity. I recall Truman Capote telling me about the wonders of cocaine as a writing aid. I think Capote's later career tells us all we need to know about that."

McInerney is an author.

APOLLO ROBBINS

ON CONFIDENCE

"About 95 percent of what I do is creating a false sense of confidence in people. The other five percent is technique. I identify what assumptions they're making, what they feel are their strong points, and enhance those aspects. I give people's confidence a little steroid boost, and I prey on that. 'This would be impossible to do to *you*, sir; you're obviously more observant than most people here.' I might be self-deprecating, so they think they understand me and know my intents, my goals. They now have a false confidence, and that's what I use. Our intuition is our vulnerability. When we automate certain tasks, we become overconfident in our ability to intuitively make decisions. If you look at Madoff, Kevin Trudeau, those types of folks, they didn't come off as grimy car salesmen—they had demeanors that empowered people's confidence."

Robbins is a sleight-of-hand artist and gentleman thief.

ANDY MURRAY

ON CONFIDENCE

"The guys with the most success, they tend to have the most confidence. But success isn't the only measure of confidence—a lot of it has to do with authenticity and how you feel about yourself. When I was younger, I used to play against a lot of kids who were older and bigger than I was, especially my brother Jamie, who always used to beat me. I think that instilled determination in me to win. It's often hard to explain a loss, and often even harder to take it, but it happens to everyone, and as long as you learn from it, the defeats can sometimes be beneficial. After I lost my first Grand Slam, I struggled with confidence. I was quite young and desperate to win a Grand Slam, and I fell short. But it didn't affect my hunger to win, and despite losing a few more finals after that, I finally won through. Perseverance and determination are key."

Murray is a tennis player.

WILLIAM
NORWICH

ON WIT

"This is the last witty thing I heard:
In the 1930s there was this place called
the Stork Club. The guy who managed
it, the big cheese, was named Sherman
Billingsley. Even though it was café
society and mixed, it was still very
snobby—let's just say that Jewish
people were kind of a new thing, and
black people were rarely seated. So the
story goes that Sherman Billingsley
arrives at his club one night and finds
Lena Horne sitting there with the
comedian George Jessel. Billingsley
walks over to the table and, looking at
Miss Horne, he very snootily says,
'Who made your reservation?' at which
point, without missing a beat, Jessel
says, 'Abraham Lincoln.' Now that's
wit. It's referential. Wit takes two to
tango. Your audience has to be smart
and informed enough to understand
the reference."

Norwich is an editor and writer.

JOYCE CAROL OATES

ON MEMORY

"The kind of writing I'm most interested in is the James Joycean approach: intensely examining a shred of memory—what the light looked like in Dublin at a certain hour on a certain day—and then filtering it through the prism of a character's consciousness, so it takes on the coloration of that mind. Our personalities are layers of memories. If you start to lose your memory, you lose your personality. It becomes cruder, a distillation of yourself. It's now known that running and walking fast are the best exercises for the brain. Neurogenesis, the regeneration of brain cells, is stimulated by running and the excitement you feel while running, which is very like the excitement of writing. I love running through a landscape—you're so alive. You're just existentially thrilled to be running. And that's why you always remember it."

Oates is an author.

MICHAEL
KORS

ON HABIT

"At the end of the day, my most consistent habit is that I'm a contradiction. There are parts of me that fully fall in the comforts, the rhythms of life. Iced tea is a constant in my hand—doesn't matter what time of day or year. When I travel to places I go to often, I always go to the same place: I think I've stayed in the same room at Claridge's in London for 20 years. I can only draw with a Sharpie and I like to sketch on lined paper; I've been sketching like that since I was a teenager. But, at the other extreme, I have the attention span of a gnat and I want something new and I'm curious about what's next. It's always a swing between the two. I've been going to Peter Luger's steakhouse since I was four, and the steak sauce there is like Proust's madeleine. But if there's a new restaurant and they're not open yet and there's no phone number, I've got to go there in the first three days. It's one extreme or the other."

Kors is a fashion designer.

WILLIAM IVEY LONG

ON TRANSFORMATION

"As a costume designer, the most obvious thing I can give an actor or an actress is a sense of structure, a sense of how to stand to create a certain appearance to others. So I begin with what's appropriate for the period and then look at the actors themselves and think, 'Well, that person slouches' or 'This person likes to stand on different legs.' They're not looking in a mirror. They have to feel it. I remember designing the black lace bodysuit that Anita Morris wore in the musical *Nine*. The first attempt was a failure. She wasn't happy, and I had to win her back. While in the fitting, a lightbulb went off. I brought in a bolt of fabric I had chosen for another costume and asked her to close her eyes. I draped it around her. When she opened her eyes, she looked at herself in the mirror and started singing. Singing! In that moment, she was the mistress. It transformed her performance."

Long is a costume designer.

MASSIMILIANO GIONI

ON TRANSFORMATION

"I was born in a relatively small town near Milan. As Italians, we tended to see a lot of art just by going to church. But I didn't even consider that art. Instead, it was a sort of visual soundtrack to religion or background noise. So my first encounters with contemporary art happened through books. One in particular, a work on pop art that I found in the town's library, was especially shocking. Later I encountered Warhol's films *Chelsea Girls* and *Trash*. These were certainly transformative experiences, but more than that, I think my early attraction to this kind of art was part of a transformative journey. I was interested in art because it was a vehicle elsewhere. Nowadays we hear a lot about contemporary art being a sort of playground for millionaires, but that's a very narrow interpretation. For me and many artists, and even some of those millionaires, art was a vehicle of both social and intellectual mobility."

Gioni is artistic director at the New Museum in New York.

MICHAEL CHOW

ON TRANSFORMATION

"In the first act of a movie, you have the 'inciting incident,' an event that brings about change in a character's life. For me, that was London. I was born in Shanghai, into a life of luxury. I was spoiled, entitled, and I hardly went to school because I was always very sick. So I was sent to school in London. This was just after the war. I was uprooted, I didn't speak the language, I had lost my culture, I knew no one, and I never saw my father again. China at the time was like North Korea is now. When I was 29, I started Mr. Chow to bridge the gap between East and West. Back then Chinese culture got zero respect. I wanted to encourage communication, focusing not just on cuisine but on an exchange between people. Suffering fuels transformation—it was that suffering early on that transformed me from a delicate little thing into someone determined to do good."

Chow is an artist and restaurateur.

BLYTHE DANNER

ON TRANSFORMATION

"I've enjoyed entering into this last chapter of life. It's been liberating. G. Stanley Hall said that old age is the only stage of life that we never grow out of, and I think that's true. The transformation into old age takes you by surprise. You never really come to terms with it, not on this earth anyway. But you look back on all of the things that you've accomplished and feel good. My children and my four grandchildren have found passion and happiness in their lives. All of that is very gratifying. But there have been some waves along the way— widowhood, for one. I never thought that would happen, that I would survive my husband, who was so strong and youthful. Still, I've never found old age to be as frightening as I think it might be for some people. Not to sound grim, but I'm not terrified of the end—it all feels like such a natural ongoing journey."

Danner is an actor.

RICHARD FORD

"Independence contains the seeds of drama—the very thing a novelist is looking for—because it always implies independence away from something. It also confers consequence on a person and a complex sense of interiority, which are also things that novelists are interested in. But does it confer strength or powerlessness? That question is part of the American narrative. A month before my novel *Independence Day* was published, I threw out the ending and wrote a new one, which we used, in which my protagonist Frank is standing beside a Fourth of July parade as it marches down the street and feeling the urge to join in. Whether or not I knew it before I started the book, I knew then for certain that the real virtue of independence was the degree to which it allows you to join the human race, rather than stand apart."

Ford is an author.

ELIZABETH OLSEN

ON ADVICE

"The most important thing to keep in mind when giving advice is an understanding of how the other person prefers to communicate. Some people like directness, while others might need you to change the tone of your voice, which might mean talking more softly or sweetly. If you approach someone in the wrong way, they're going to have a closed-off response, so it's necessary to remain sensitive to their needs. I think I'm pretty good at giving and receiving advice—although I bet I'm pretty bad at it as well!—but sometimes you have to take what's said with a grain of salt, because a piece of advice can be based on whatever mood a person is in that day, and it's always limited to an individual's own experience. Sometimes your gut reaction is an important one. It can be the best way to go."

Olsen is an actor.

AMY CHUA

ON OBSESSION

"Obsessive people tend not to be very good at leading happy, balanced lives, and they're not very fun to be around. They're tormented. But at the same time, obsessions are responsible for so much of human greatness and accomplishment throughout history: Michelangelo, Beethoven, Einstein, Steve Jobs. How many people who have changed history would you describe as 'chill'? What obsession gives people is an almost pathological focus and single-mindedness. But sometimes the success that obsession generates can come at the cost of others. I became a little obsessed with making my two daughters realize their potential with their piano and violin playing. But even now my daughter will say, 'Wow, I can't believe I played the Mendelssohn concerto at 13.' There is satisfaction, a real feeling of joy and fulfillment, in the product of obsession that I think people underestimate."

Chua is a Yale law professor and author.

ANNA NETREBKO

ON OBSESSION

"Obsession is a kind of sick thing, I
think. It's not a very positive word for
me. The people who are driven by
obsession tend to be very sensitive
people and very strong in a way, but
also weak because they cannot protect
themselves. Obsession can really ruin
a personality and the person themselves. I guess it's good to experience,
but it's even better if you stay away
from it. The fact is, if you're really
dying to have something, it's usually
sort of running away from you.
Obsession occurs for me when I fall in
love. It's horrible. I hate it. It's like a
sickness—you can't do anything, you
only think about that one thing. You're
waiting for phone calls. It can be
beautiful, but I don't like to be weak—
I don't like to be under the control of
something else. When you are
obsessed and in love, you're silly and
stupid, and your whole life stops
around you. I like being in control—
I have too many things to do."

Netrebko is an opera singer.

MAIRA
KALMAN
ON YOUTH

"For me, writing children's books was
the result of having children: the
antics, the divine mayhem, the
imagination, the wonderful
conversation all propelled me to want
to make books and write. With
children's books, you can take chances
and experiment and be silly. There is
no expectation to be correct. To be able
to be wrong is such an incredible gift
and luxury. You're not supposed to be
wrong when you're an adult, doing
adult work. There are things that need
to be done and rules that need to be
followed. But in children's books, you
can be stupid and smart and confused
and overconfident. I wander around
and I show what the world looks like
through my eyes. As my son told me
today, I'm still a 6-year-old. It's
amazing work, amazing fun—when I'm
not crying."

Kalman is a writer and illustrator.

DWYANE WADE
ON DISCIPLINE

"When you realize what matters most to you, that's when you understand how to discipline yourself. You're not going to always have people telling you yea or nay. When you're an athlete and in the limelight, people feel like they can't tell you certain things. You have to be disciplined on your own. I had to learn to check myself as I understood there weren't a lot of people who were going to tell me when I was doing things wrong. Being disciplined is being a professional, understanding that I have a job to do and knowing that I'm not walking around worried about just me. It's my three boys, Zaire and Zion and Dahveon, who I'm concerned about. The first thing— morning, noon, night—is them. Getting custody of my sons and deciding to raise my nephew, that was the most disciplined moment in my life."

Wade is an NBA basketball player.

ANTONIA FRASER

ON SOLITUDE

"I think the mother of six children has an important relationship with solitude. To put it mildly, solitude to write—and I do need to write alone—is one of the most precious things. I'm also the oldest of eight children, and long before I read Virginia Woolf and *A Room of One's Own*, the greatest luxury I had was to have a room of my own. I think I had a sort of jealous attitude toward solitude from the start. My former husband Harold Pinter was an only child. He was much less jealous of solitude because he had had so much more of it than me. I started to write my memoir, *Must You Go?*, a month after he died. By writing it I was no longer alone, because I was writing about us. That memoir was a reaction to this unchosen solitude. [Percy Bysshe] Shelley, I think, is extraordinary on solitude: 'I love all waste and solitary places; where we taste the pleasure of believing what we see is boundless, as we wish our souls to be.'"

Fraser is an author, biographer and historian.

KITTY KELLEY

ON SECRETS

"In writing about the lives of other people, I've learned that we all have secrets, and keeping them is what drives a life—it can either darken or illuminate it. I started writing biographies because the lives of people who have influenced our culture fascinate me. Most of those individuals have public images fashioned by major public relations firms, but I wanted to go *behind* the fairy tale. What are they really like? How have they exerted their power? There's certainly room on the shelf for both authorized and unauthorized biographies. I've written about Frank Sinatra—as a child in Hoboken, he knew great shame because his mother performed abortions—and also the Kennedys and the Reagans. Not every secret leads to dysfunction; some secrets can lead to good once they're revealed. I truly believe that you are as sick as your secret—and I'd like to make everybody well."

Kelley is a journalist and biographer.

DIMITRI DIMITROV

ON SECRETS

"Before I came to Sunset Tower, I was running Diaghilev, a Russian restaurant in West Hollywood, an under-the-radar place where Tom Cruise, Sean Penn and Tom Ford were regulars. At Tower Bar too, all kinds of people come; secrecy is part of what we do. Manners and behavior matter a lot to me—I'm old school. When our clients see me standing out front, they know what to expect. Whenever Johnny Depp is in town, he might come to Sunset Tower to have a meeting with family or his producer, but no one knows he's there. Gossip magazines have tried to buy me half a dozen times, and each time I tell them never to bother me again. These are important people. It's their night, and there's no room for paparazzi. And it's not only celebrities, it's doctors, lawyers, agents. It's not my business whether they're with a girlfriend, a wife or a mistress. It's a day-and-night job. Privacy is key."

Dimitrov is a maître d'hôtel.

MIRA NAIR

ON ENVY

"Envy is a corrosive thing. It weaves
its ugly magic. But it is also a fact of
life. Hollywood and the world often
feed us this lie, which is that only one
of us can succeed at a time—us being
women or people of color or any 'other.'
We are told both subliminally and
directly that there is not enough room
for all of us, that there is a limit of *one*
success story. This lie creates envy and
divides those who should be in
solidarity. But I reject this lie. Envy is
utterly useless. We must teach
ourselves to see through it, because
it's such a game. It's not a propulsive
thing. We cannot succeed alone.
True success comes only when we are
all lifted. Still, envy is fertile ground
for creative work. We are drawn to it
because it reveals the prismatic human
being. A person who is envious is not a
bad person—there is much more to it
than that. There is no gorgeous drama
in everything being good."

Nair is a director.

DANI SHAPIRO

ON LANGUAGE

"Words are our primary means of communication, but they are limited in terms of eliciting an emotional response. When we listen to a glorious symphony, it pierces us—there's something in it that inexplicably and wordlessly moves us. Part of the job of the writer is to attempt to use words in a way that creates that same wordless feeling of having one's world rocked. I don't tend to write about politics, but in recent months I've found myself worrying about the state of the world. Writers are their own instruments, so when that instrument changes, as it's changing in this moment, it feels urgently important to understand how to tune it. I teach creative writing to people trying to know themselves better, to open themselves up to the contents of their own inner lives using language—and *that*, I've lately been feeling, is a political act."

Shapiro is an author.

R. L. STINE

"I'm not interested in *really* scaring kids—that was a decision I made early on. It's just all about entertainment, a creepy adventure. I read mysteries and thrillers, but I hate the Scandinavian stuff. It's so earnest and humorless. There's such a close connection between horror and humor, but no one in those books ever cracks a joke! The chapters in my work all end on a cliffhanger, and for me that's like writing a punch line. But it's a challenge now. Kids are smarter because of all the technology. Still, no matter the technology, fear stays the same. The *Goosebumps* books probably could have been written when I was a kid in the '50s, because it's the same stuff that was going on in all the horror movies that my brother and I used to go to every Saturday—the fear of going into the dark or of something lurking under your bed."

Stine is an author.

OZZY OSBOURNE

ON FEAR

"We used to rehearse opposite a movie theater. I think it was Tony [Iommi] or Geezer [Butler] who said, 'Isn't it strange the way people pay money to go and get scared? Why don't we start doing scary music?' At the time, we were playing jazz blues. Everything else was all bubble gum and flower power. There was that song that went, 'If you're going to San Francisco, be sure to wear some flowers in your hair.' Well, for four guys coming from Aston in Birmingham [England], which was bombed in the war, still cold and wet and a major industrial place— it wasn't San Francisco to us. It was bulls—t, really. That's all it was. We didn't even realize that black magic was a thing people actually practiced! We just wanted to be scary."

Osbourne is a musician and the lead singer of Black Sabbath.

YOKO
ONO

ON PATIENCE

"There was one thing both my husband, John, and I didn't know about each other until we got together: how totally mercurial we were. John was mercurially loud, and I was mercurially silent. We were a match. John and I felt that we were like people in an H. G. Wells story. Two people who are walking so fast that nobody else can see them. The lonely ones, who laugh and throw kisses to each other in the mirror. For people like us, a patient is a sick person in a hospital. Have patience and you'll be sick. When you're flying, let yourself keep flying. Don't stop. A word like 'patience' will only make you stop flying and fall—wings and all."

Ono is an artist and musician.

THOM
BROWNE

ON FATE

"I think about fate and fulfilling my own destiny often. It's what brought me to what I do now. Fate is just your predetermined destiny, but, unlike destiny, you have no control over it. That's what makes life special and, at times, challenging. But luck is important too. You can work really hard to get to a certain point, but you have no control over luck, which may or may not be in your favor. But fate isn't so black and white. I think my fate was, not to sound self-congratulatory, to be good at something. Obviously it wasn't acting! My destiny was to become a fashion designer. I found something I liked, so I worked incredibly hard at trying to be the best at it. Yes, my work feels fated, but the ideas come from somewhere. Ultimately, it's about creating something on your own, creating something for yourself. *You* make it happen for yourself."

Browne is a fashion designer.

PAULA
HAWKINS

ON FATE

"I don't believe in fate in the sense of there being some power or agency that orders the course of events. There are all sorts of terrible things that can happen to you that you have no control over. But I understand how fatalism, the sense that certain things are meant to be, can be quite comforting at those times. And perhaps the idea that I'm the master of my own fate is just another sort of artificial comfort. The sort of crimes I'm interested in writing about tend to involve a lot of random elements and coincidence. People just happen to come across each other at precisely the wrong points in their lives. Even my career seems to hinge on randomness. Obviously you work hard and try your best, but in terms of this kind of success, it comes down largely to chance."

Hawkins is an author.

JOSH OSTROVSKY

ON FATE

"I like the unpredictability of life. I'm a big fan of the fact that we're on a giant rock hurtling through outer space at like a billion miles per hour, that we're just a bunch of talking dots. That's kind of crazy and scary to think about, but I embrace that fear. I'm all for a little bit of disaster—that's part of what I do professionally and personally. I like getting up every day not knowing where I'm waking up, who I'm waking up next to or what's going to happen during that day. The notion of being in control at all times just doesn't sound appealing. It's interesting to let the world abduct you and take you hostage for a minute and see where you come out on the other side. Could that all be fate? I guess. But I think it takes away from your awesomeness and your raw humanness to say that everything was predetermined."

Ostrovsky, aka the Fat Jew, is a comedian and social media personality.

ERTHARIN COUSIN

ON FATE

"One of the things that my family gave me was faith. I believe that we have a God who takes care of all of us. But I also believe man can put obstacles in the way of our faith and our future. Fate is always impacted by opportunities. Without having the tools to walk through a door, even when that door is opened, you will not have the opportunity to live life to its full potential. I grew up on the west side of Chicago, the inner city. There was nothing about it that hinted at where I would be today, working to feed people around the world. Some might say it was my fate. I would say, yes, it was my fate, but it was also my faith, my education, my parents—it was standing on the shoulders of individuals who opened doors for me, people I knew and didn't know."

Cousin is a distinguished fellow of global agriculture at the Chicago Council on Global Affairs.

RON HOWARD

ON IMPULSE

"Over the course of my career, I have impulsively agreed to four projects. I didn't do the things that I normally do, I didn't talk to Brian Grazer or my wife, I didn't agonize over the decision. Now, I would go to my grave with two of those projects. But the other two? I wish I could get the months I invested in them back. But I enjoy taking risks—I'm not remotely interested in becoming more conservative in my choices as I get older. You come to embrace impulsiveness more when you're working on live-action productions. I encourage actors to take those creative leaps, too. But it's important to understand where impulsive behavior fits into your strategy and life. One person's impulses may be gold, while they may be someone else's Achilles' heel. Do you have a golden gut? Does your temper get you into trouble? It's wise to make a conscious effort to reflect and do the math."

Howard is a film director.

PAT MCGRATH

ON TRANSFORMATION

"My mother was a keen follower of all things related to fashion and beauty. She trained me at a young age—everything from looking at the patterns to checking the fabrics and scrutinizing the look for the makeup. She would even quiz me on different shades of eye shadows! Her obsession with cosmetics came from a combination of thrift and the lack of available makeup for dark skin, which fueled her creativity. Back then, we might find one shadow color per month that worked with our pigmentation. So we would mix them together.

It would be naive not to acknowledge the pressures women are faced with to look a certain way. But for me, a bit of makeup has always been a way to gain an instant confidence boost. People can benefit from the unique personal transformation that makeup can provide, because when you paint your face up to exude confidence, it often works inward."

McGrath is a makeup artist.

ROY BAUMEISTER

ON WILLPOWER

"We need to understand willpower as a limited energy. The human willpower glass is very much half full and half empty. We get a lot more than other creatures do, and it's contributed immensely to the success of our species. But I think there's also the sense that if we had a little more, we would do even better. I call self-control the moral muscle. It's what creates the capacity for humans to act in certain ways when they don't want to. So what we need to understand is that we have this marvelous capacity but that it is not unlimited. It fails sometimes. The key is that self-control works through habits. By setting up good habits, you're not resisting temptation or getting yourself out of jams or fighting the odds, but rather you're using your self-control to set life up to run on autopilot. Then it runs smoothly, and you can save your willpower to put into more creative endeavors."

Baumeister is an author and psychology professor at Florida State University.

TRACY ANDERSON

ON WILLPOWER

"I think willpower is something that we all have, but it has to be ignited. Willpower requires you to be straight with and have tough conversations with yourself. You have to really figure out where the imbalances are in your life and fix them. You can make excuses for why you needed the candy in the office or why you couldn't get your workout in, but they're just not true. The willpower behind doing a juice cleanse for seven days to get bikini-ready is the wrong kind—it's driven by vanity. The better kind is driven by a vision of what the human body can do with focus and achievement. Music helps—it's the classic tool for pumping yourself up. I put on Eminem's "Not Afraid" and I'm like, This is right: I'm not stopping, I'm not folding, I'm not derailing here. And a Van Halen song can get me through just about anything."

Anderson is a personal trainer and fitness entrepreneur.

MEB KEFLEZIGHI

ON WILLPOWER

"Willpower is something you practice daily. You don't come to the exam unprepared. In training, you have a dialogue with yourself: I think I'm ready with speed, with race pace— I think I can cover the distance. After the London Olympics, where I didn't win a medal, I was in a wheel- chair. I put everything on the line—my feet were brutally blistered from the cobblestones. I was not prepared. But after finishing fourth, I also knew internally that I could win New York or Boston. At Boston in 2014 I'd been told that I was too old. At 17 miles, I remember making the right turn at the Newton fire station. I'd just run a 4:31 mile, my foot was aching badly. But I was like, 'Ignore the pain. You are carrying the nation on your back. This is for Boston. This is for the United States. Just stick to it.' You can't win every race, but you just have to dig deep and keep digging."

Keflezighi is a retired long-distance runner. He won the Boston Marathon in 2014 at the age of 38.

ANNE W. RIMOIN

ON RISK

"When your life's work is studying emerging infectious diseases in the remote jungles of the Democratic Republic of the Congo, risk is relative. My family, friends and colleagues often ask me, 'Aren't you scared about contracting a disease?' The truth is I am not particularly worried about catching a virus while investigating cases of monkeypox or viral hemorrhagic fevers, because I am extremely careful and take the necessary precautions to protect my team and myself. I am much more concerned about the dangers associated with driving or flying in the Congo, which has one of the worst accident records in the world. Unfortunately, the places that require the most risk to access are generally also those where the need for public health assistance is the greatest. For me, the possibility of stopping the next pandemic before it starts is well worth the risk."

Rimoin is an infectious disease epidemiologist.

CHRISTINA TOSI

ON INNOVATION

"One of the ways I hang on to creative or innovative ideas is by being a lunatic about notes. I have a desk, a laptop, notebooks, loose papers littered with Post-its, notes written on the backs of business cards, even written on cardboard ripped from a box. I always try to organize the process so I feel like less of a lunatic, but oftentimes something just bursts out of my head and I know if I don't capture it immediately, it will disappear. So I embrace the craziness and grab whatever is closest—which is sometimes a Sharpie in someone's apron or a pen in someone's ponytail—and scribble on whatever is close by. But at the same time, when it comes to innovation, there's a beauty to limiting yourself: backing yourself into a corner to force your creative mind back into itself until it implodes into something exponentially greater than it once was—kind of like nuclear energy."

Tosi is the chef, founder and owner of Momofuku Milk Bar.

BRUNELLO
CUCINELLI

ON LOYALTY

"I've always been attracted to the humanistic concept of loyalty—an emphasis on respect for everyone's dignity. To be loyal doesn't only mean to fulfill commitments to others; it's something more. We should care for our neighbors, yes, but others as well, even strangers. We should be loyal to everybody. That loyalty enables us to join forces to serve what we like to refer to as 'the common good.' Loyalty features prominently in my business. This is exactly the reason why we almost never change our workers and clients. When I restored the parks around the small village of Solomeo in Italy—where our company is head-quartered and my wife was born—I did it out of a sense of responsibility and loyalty to the people in the town. I want them to feel proud of the place where they live and work."

Cucinelli is a fashion designer.

SARAH
PAULSON

ON LOYALTY

"As an actor, loyalty to your character and her story is of paramount impor-tance. I will never stand in judgment of any character I play. You can't abandon them, no matter what they do, think or feel. It serves me not one bit, and it doesn't serve the story. Mistress Epps [from *12 Years a Slave*] was a diabolical character—her behavior was reprehen-sible. But I remember [director] Steve McQueen telling me, 'You must not judge her.' So I didn't look for ways to excuse her behavior. Instead, I tried to understand her actions within the context of her time. She wasn't smart enough to question what she'd been told; she wasn't an independent person of mind or heart. But the story wouldn't be told in the same way if I'd tried to make her more palatable. My job is to serve the story, and if you have no loyalty to your character, you might as well not bother."

Paulson is an actor.

MARTINE
ROTHBLATT
ON LOYALTY

"Phyllis Frye, a transgender judge in Houston, once made the point that if you're transgender and you're able to be a good role model to others, that's something you have to do out of loyalty to your tribe. Otherwise, people will continue to live these sad, closeted lives. I've been really lucky. I would never have come out if my partner had not been 100 percent behind me, loyal to me, because I love her more than I love myself. There are many instances when the relationship does not survive after one partner comes out as transgender, but mine was not one of them. In that way, loyalty is related to love. I like how Robert Heinlein, the science fiction writer, defined love: The happiness of the person you love is essential to your own happiness. In the case of loyalty, the happiness of the person you are loyal to is important to your own happiness."

Rothblatt is founder and CEO of United Therapeutics and founder of Sirius radio.

T. C. BOYLE

ON AMBITION

"Ambition for artists is like life on this earth: It's self-replicating and there's no end to it. All of us, especially novelists, are damaged, psychologically damaged. We have big problems, and we are not good people. We're drug addicts, we're drunks. So we want to even the score— we want adulation. If you are single-minded, as many writers are, as I am, the work is all you are. There is nothing else. And so if the work goes away, then it's the gun. We've seen it through generations of American writers. That is the downside to ambition. When I was a student at Iowa Writers' Workshop, I remember old writers would say, 'Why you're doing this is for the doing of it itself, for its own value and for yourself.' And I thought privately, 'Well, what horse s—t.' But now that I'm an old writer, I've realized that it is true."

Boyle is an author.

SARAH SZE

ON OBSESSION

"In the creative process, obsession changes linear time. You become entirely engrossed: Time becomes lost, elastic, and things shift and glide in ways that we don't usually experience in the world. It's not only when you're creating but also when you're experiencing art, like a piece of music you're obsessed with. That's why people become addicted to the creative process. This kind of obsession has nothing to do with anxiety and in many ways is a relief from anxiety. When I start to dream about a piece of art I'm working on, that's when I know I'm in the middle of an interesting process. I've lately become sort of obsessed by Chris Marker's movie *La Jetée*. It's about a person who's obsessed with an image of his past, and because he's so obsessed, people can use him as a tool for time travel. I love this idea that obsession liberates you from linear time and allows you to become a vehicle for something else."

Sze is an artist.

FRANCIS CHOLLE

ON INTUITION

"I do not believe in looking at intuition as an instrument that makes black-and-white decisions. It's a balance between two instruments. One weighs what's heavier, lighter, taller, shorter. That's the rational mind. The other goes to the depths of the ocean and comes back with information from under the radar of reason. It's like a radio that's always on. We either tune in or we don't. The more you grow up, the more you learn that you can't control life, that not everything makes sense—and that deep down we are more irrational than rational. If you don't trust your ability to evaluate and engage the irrational part of a human being, you set yourself up for failure. If you only go by logical plans—profitability, structure, rational conversation—you remove emotion, instinct and the ability to evolve and invent. You disconnect yourself from your best instrument for adaptability, creativity and performance."

Cholle is a business consultant and author.

SUSAN MILLER

ON INTUITION

"Our culture emphasizes the factual, rational, analytical side of the brain, but sometimes does so to our detriment. The ancient astrologers gave equal importance to both sides of the brain: the analytical and the intuitive. They felt that if we were to ignore or mistrust the intuitive side, we would not be able to access all the tools available to us to adeptly navigate life. Relying on one's intuition requires self-confidence, for at first you have little information to confirm what it's telling you. But have faith—those facts will surface later. If you don't act on the signals of your intuition, often those messages will grow louder until they become impossible to ignore. Some people are uncomfortable making decisions in the face of ambiguity, but others, often those who ascend to leadership positions, are very comfortable doing so. Those prescient souls know that in life we can't always have things 'just so.'"

Miller is an astrologer.

CHRISTOPHER GUEST

ON INTUITION

"I suppose my work is where intuition is literally invaluable. In my normal life, when I'm driving my son to school, it doesn't have quite the same impact—except if I saw an alien ship landing on the freeway, my instinct would say, Maybe get off one exit earlier. But there's nothing practical about what I do for work. I guess you could say it's entirely intuition. There's no dialogue written down for the actors, so when I interview, I just talk with them for 15 minutes and then ask myself whether I imagine they can do this work. Improvisation is one of those things that you either can do or can't. It's very much an effort where everyone is playing together. It's not about soloing all the time. There's no test, but it's like sitting down with a musician and starting to play. It's instantly apparent what's going on and if that's going to be a good thing."

Guest is a screenwriter and director.

DANIELLE STEEL

ON INTUITION

"I think there are two very important components of intuition: listening to and hearing that intuition; and then trusting it. There is another kind of false intuition based on anxiety, fear, superstition or even panic, which can be confusing. But quietly listening to our intuition can serve us well. My intuition has developed over time. When I was younger, I didn't listen to it and rarely trusted it. I have enough faith in myself now to trust what my instincts tell me and even to look foolish if others don't agree. The best advice I have ever given my children is to 'listen to your gut.' Hear it, trust it. Deep in our hearts we almost always know what is right for us and what we should be doing."

Steel is an author.

TOM
SELLECK

ON LUCK

"If you're going to pursue something, you should start where you might be the luckiest. I talk with a lot of young actors, and I tell them, 'You're going to get lucky soon so you better be prepared. When you get a big break, you're going to lose 25 percent of your talent to nerves because you want the job so much. So you better be overqualified. Develop an appetite for failure, because it's either going to defeat you or it will teach you. There's a time, and it comes to all of us, when the phone stops ringing. It's a very tricky business, because the product that is being rejected is you, not a refrigerator. The disappointments are huge. The closer you get to being lucky, the bigger the disappointments will be when you're not. You can call it character, you can call it perseverance, but if you want to get lucky, stay at it.'"

Selleck is an actor.

SUSAN WOJCICKI

ON POPULARITY

"To be popular means to be admired by a specific group. It's different from fame, which points to a broader fan base and suggests that you earned recognition through some kind of notable achievement. The common definition of *popularity* may bring up a negative idea of high school: exclusiveness, cliques, beautiful people and mean girls. But popularity has a different meaning when it relates to media. In that arena, it's positive; it means something is a hit. In regard to social media, one significant force of determining who is popular is this idea of authenticity—it's the common denominator among popular YouTube creators. In many ways, authenticity gives a creator a richer set of dimensions, more than we might have seen with traditional media stars of the past who may be more concerned with a perfect, glossy image."

Wojcicki is CEO of YouTube.

CAL RIPKEN JR.

ON ADMIRATION

"When you're successful in baseball, or almost any other sport, you may become a source of admiration for others. It's definitely an adjustment, and I've seen people react to it in different ways. It may go to one's head and breed arrogance, for instance. But I've always tried to maintain perspective—I think that was part of my dad's influence on me. The ability to hit or catch or run is just another skill, and we all have skills, but it doesn't make you better than anyone else. Brooks Robinson is one of my favorite baseball players, and one thing that struck me about him was that he always seemed to have time for everyone. Sure, you want to be a good baseball player, but you also must remember to be a good person. And just as it's important to maintain perspective as someone in my position, it's also important to maintain perspective when admiring someone else—because they're just a person, too."

Ripken is a philanthropist and a former professional baseball player.

ALICE WATERS

ON EPIPHANIES

"Twenty years ago, I was quoted in a newspaper complaining about the look of a local Berkeley school—the lawn was burnt out, the windows had graffiti on them. Well, the principal called me. I visited the school and we walked around. It was built in 1922 for 500 kids—now there were nearly 1,000. We came upon a large area; all at once, I saw a garden there instead of an abandoned lot. And then there was a little shack in the back where I envisioned an enormous cafeteria, one that could seat every child, where they could eat for free. I've always felt that a table can be a place of true equality in America. Everyone sits and eats together. I never thought of the garden as simply providing food for the cafeteria, but instead a place where the children could learn. Of course, my idea eventually grew into the Edible Schoolyard Project, which now has reach all around the world. But it all began with that one epiphany."

Waters is a chef, restaurateur and creator of the Edible Schoolyard Project.

CHERYL BOONE ISAACS

ON PROGRESS

"Everything has a yin and yang. Cracking the atom opened up a world of possibilities in science, but then that knowledge was used to create a weapon of mass destruction. But progress is inevitable. I've been in the entertainment business for quite a long time, and we've progressed quite a bit in regards to diversity. Right now, there's an ongoing conversation about how to be more inclusive of all the talent available in the U.S. and around the world. We've made some strides, but we're just at the beginning of that conversation. When the Academy nominated *Selma* for best picture, it showed a major regard for the talent that it took to make that movie. But no matter the advancements, what will always remain is storytelling— whether it's drawings on the side of a cave or *Jurassic World* today. As we move forward, we'll only continue to see different stories."

Isaacs is the 35th president of the Academy of Motion Picture Arts and Sciences.

DAVID MUIR

ON PROGRESS

"Broadcast now is sort of a living, breathing thing that evolves all day long. The stakes are much higher at 6:30 p.m. because people are engaged in the news from the moment they wake up. They check their iPhones and see the headlines. Given the tools of social media, there are so many individuals who have a voice now who didn't have a voice before. My first week in the anchor chair we went to the Syrian border and reported on a little girl who hadn't gone to school for years—she was a refugee—working instead six or seven hours in the fields. Viewers responded within 24 hours of the report, donating enough money to supply 2,200 classrooms. We revisited her in a follow-up segment. Now at the end of her workday she skips across the fields to attend a makeshift school. It's a reminder to us that we can connect people with what's happening a world away."

Muir is a journalist and the anchor of ABC World News Tonight.

DANIELLE BROOKS

ON PROGRESS

"I had just graduated from Juilliard when I booked *Orange Is the New Black*. I was trying to understand how I fit in Hollywood. Do I need to straighten my hair for auditions? Do I need to lose weight? It's very challenging as a young actress to figure out how to make it in an industry where all of your examples don't look like you. What I started realizing was that there was a lack of diversity among the higher-ups, the people in the suits, so it did not trickle down as quickly. When *Orange* came out, it was such a gift to me. I feel a responsibility to do great work. I feel a responsibility to strive for projects that don't keep women in a box, to constantly push and challenge how people view me as a person and the roles that I can play. A part of progress is perseverance, a nothing-can-stop-you kind of attitude. We're in a time where people are done accepting the minimum. We'll continue to see change. It's past due."

Brooks is an actor.

JULIAN FELLOWES

ON INDULGENCE

"Cold weather is always a good background for stuffing yourself with food. In the old days, houses were very cold compared to the way we live now, no matter how well-off people were. They couldn't stroll around inside in a T-shirt and jeans in the middle of December because they'd freeze to death. The feasting, the roaring fire, the mulled wine, the hot roast were all ways of combating that. A summer feast is a lighter thing: cold salmon, mayonnaise, a salad. It's charming but there's not quite the same sense of vice that a really good feed in the winter gives you. I'm one of those people who loves the Christmas menu. I want to have the turkey, roast potatoes, sprouts, stuffing, wine and good champagne—all of it. I'm afraid it's a big weight putter-onner, and since I'm already as fat as a barrel, I almost dread the coming of the season, for I know I will be able to resist none of it."

Fellowes is an actor, novelist, producer, director and screenwriter.

MARINA ABRAMOVIC
ON DISCIPLINE

"I would like to create more space and have more time to do nothing. Art history is filled with examples of artists who have fought their entire lives for their work and their beliefs. To create unique energy you have to be disciplined. But it's also important to learn how not to let this energy destroy you. I have very strong work habits, but when I decide to take a rest, I'm also a master at doing nothing without guilt. When you create, the higher the euphoria of creation, the lower you can fall in your private life. I made up the term 'body drama' to describe this idea. It's like when you see a rock group singing to thousands and thousands of listeners. The audience gives all of its energy to the performer. It inflates the ego. Once the concert is finished, that energy can destroy. It's why so many great performers are brought down by drugs or alcohol. This is why discipline is essential."

Abramovic is an artist.

MARY BOONE

ON AMBITION

"Contrary to most thinking, the dictionary definition of *ambition* is actually fairly benign. It's a desire to work hard in order to achieve something. It's funny that the connotation of ambition has turned out to be a bit more cutthroat, almost negative. It's particularly controversial when it's attached to women. When I thought of ambition in my 20s as I started being a young art dealer, I thought of Leo Castelli, men, money and power. It was very daunting. At that age you always wonder, Is there going to be room for me? Is my statement valuable enough? And now, when I think of ambition, I think how great it is that I'm in a field with all these incredible, powerful, beautiful, smart women, like Marian Goodman, Helene Winer, Janelle Reiring and Barbara Gladstone. Ambition is something that more and more women are feeling comfortable with. "

Boone is an art dealer.

JANICE MIN
ON AMBITION

"After editing so many profiles and interviews over the years, I've found that the most ambitious people are usually far from ordinary. They've oftentimes overcome childhood trauma or grown up in dysfunctional families or had addictions. I've come to believe that ambition is an overcompensation for a feeling that life may have disappointed them early on. Celebrities often come from a deep place of need. You look at someone like Channing Tatum—you get the sense that he had a pretty rough youth, and he's so ambitious and not afraid to be ambitious. We're in such a competitive business landscape right now; no one wants a slacker on his or her hands. So the ability to express and project ambition is probably more desired now than it ever has been. It's not a dirty word. We live in a pretty transparent time."

Min is an editor and writer.

ANNE
PASTERNAK

ON VULNERABILITY

"*Vulnerability* could be the word for
our time. I think if you were to name
this period it could easily be called the
Vulnerability Era because there are
people who are feeling vulnerable,
insecure and fearful right now.
For example, if you're a Muslim in this
country or many places around the
world, you're feeling vulnerable.
Women are feeling vulnerable about
the rights they have fought for with
regards to health care. So when I think
about vulnerability I think about
larger issues of social unrest. But I
don't shut these feelings down—I'm
open to them, and it becomes a source
of inspiration for programs at the
museum. I'm a big believer that our
cultural institutions are places for us
not only to come in and learn about our
past but to question and hear one
another's stories, to be exposed to one
another's histories and beliefs."

*Pasternak is the director of the Brooklyn
Museum in New York City.*

THOM
MAYNE
ON LANGUAGE

"In any specialized territory, you have a somewhat private language used in-house. In architecture, for instance, there are terms we use like *building envelope*—that's literally the skin of a building. The language evolves as the work evolves, once we attempt to articulate it. It's necessary to find descriptions that are useful among specialists, because we're dealing with it at a much more specific, idiosyncratic level. It's not even about efficiency—it's trying to find words that deal with the conceptual nature of our discipline. There used to be many more architecture critics, especially at newspapers. They proved immensely important because they translated your voice into one that connected with an audience. Architects miss those critics because they explained to the outside world how a building is used, how it connects socially or culturally or politically, in terms other than our own."

Mayne is an architect.

HODA KOTB
ON FEAR

"I don't know how epiphanies happen, but they happen. I was in my apartment—this was after I got sick [with breast cancer]—when I had this feeling. I heard four words: 'You can't scare me.' All at once, everything I had been afraid of seemed so small. Around that time I learned that they were going to add a fourth hour to *Today*. I had never asked for a promotion—I was the one who sat down, who knew if I worked hard someone would notice. It had served me fine in my career, but I remember saying to myself, 'I'm going to ask for this job.' So I took the elevator to Jeff Zucker's office. I was so calm. It seemed like *nothing*. Someone had just told me I had more years to live! So I went in there and gave this speech. I'm sure he thought I was crazy with the 'I had this epiphany; you can't scare me.' But if I hadn't gotten sick, I wouldn't have gotten the job—I would have been too scared. But I did it!"

Kotb is a coanchor of NBC's Today Show.

CHLOË GRACE MORETZ
ON FEAR

"I've had the amazing opportunity to work consistently since I was 12 years old. I haven't taken more than a month off from work. It's been really humbling. But all of that comes with fame, and fame is terrifying. It's terrifying to think that when you walk down the street people will know you, know what you like to eat in the morning—or, at least, they think they know you. And then, of course, there's fear of the paparazzi. You lose your anonymity. But it all goes hand in hand with fame. It's why people buy tickets to the movies. But if you're not careful, it can take a hold of you. What scares me even more, though, is the idea that one day this might be something I won't love, to think that there could be a time that this no longer makes me happy—because, as of now, this is the biggest love of my life. I don't ever want to get to that spot."

Moretz is an actor.

MIRANDA JULY

ON COURAGE

"You read in the newspaper about something unendurable that's happened and you think, I don't know how people are surviving that. But the truth is—and you know this if you've been in a really hard situation—you don't have a choice. Those people are just like you. They just don't have a choice. You don't just suddenly become a saint, filled with courage because fate has dealt this hand to you. It's more like, what are you going to do? You have to be strong; you have no options. In my relationship with my husband, I'm pretty good in emergencies. I think the reason for that is in my household growing up we were kind of in a state of emergency all the time. So when something's actually happening, I almost relax. I admire my husband because he has a kind of daily courage, an ability not to get bogged down in all the anxieties and depressions that can come up in a day. To me, that seems so brave."

July is an artist and filmmaker.

MAYA GABEIRA

ON COURAGE

"When I was starting to surf growing up, I was frightened by waves—I was very scared. I was extremely intimidated, because I was not a good swimmer. But my confidence really built with time, along with my passion, determination and learning. I think everyone has that ability within themselves to be courageous. It's a matter of exercising it and applying it in life. Knowledge helps a lot too. A lot of people experience an uncomfortable feeling about being in the ocean because it's very powerful and it's an unknown for them. You need a lot of experience to understand and read the ocean. Part of understanding the ocean is knowing your limits. The challenge we have in big-wave surfing is you want to perform at your very best when the waves are huge, but we're all scared of drowning. It's about how to find waves, being as safe as possible and wanting to take the risk. The reward is in that as well."

Gabeira is a professional big-wave surfer.

FRANÇOIS NARS

ON COLOR

"I have never believed in rules when it comes to makeup. Sometimes the most dissonant color combinations can be the most interesting. I always encourage women to experiment with bold color in the way they might experiment with colorful accessories. What I do recommend is keeping everything in moderation, and if you're going to experiment with color on the face, make sure you blend. We are not afraid to be a bit different— to make shades that are unexpected. Color never exists in a void; the secret is contrast. When I create makeup shades, I like honest, bold colors, almost flashy. I invented the color Orgasm as a blush shade in 1999. Looking back, I think the combination of the name and the shade made it so popular. It's both cool and warm, peach and pink, with a pop of shimmer for a natural flush of color and highlight. For me, color and light go hand in hand. All colors can be amazing in the right context— I couldn't choose one as a favorite."

Nars is the founder of Nars, a cosmetics company.

GOLDIE HAWN

ON YOUTH

"The childlike part of being an actor is a wonderful thing. The act of pretending, dressing up like someone else in hair and makeup, replacing yourself—it's make-believe. That tool needs to be honed and exercised for the rest of your life. It's the quality that constitutes wonder, that helps you to realize 'yes' is always a better answer, to go out and do things with bravery and fearlessness, and it creates more energy around you. We get older every day, but youth is a state of mind. That was the thing about *Death Becomes Her*—I thought it was an incredibly prophetic film. It asks, 'What would happen if we lived forever?' And the reality is, it would be terrible! Finding love and getting older and sharing the stages of life as we move through them is probably the most important thing we can learn to do."

Hawn is an actor.

CLAIRE MESSUD

ON STATUS QUO

"I grew up with all these contradictory messages when it came to the status quo and how it related to the lives of girls and women. My mother was an active feminist in her reading and the things she said to us, and yet in her daily life she was a traditional wife—she married in the '50s and was still living in the '50s in the '90s. I adored my dad, but I don't believe he ever boiled an egg. So that question— what is the status quo?—was always fairly complicated. Certainly, they were specific concerns in my novel *The Woman Upstairs*, in terms of Nora's desire to be an artist and the ways in which all those contradictions play out in her life. But I would say an interest in the messy reality of those contradictions is something that I've internalized. That's been part of my experience my whole life, not only with my family, but in watching other people's lives."

Messud is an author.

LOUISE
FISHMAN
ON STATUS QUO

"Status quo is something that you think exists, but it's just a framework for how we live, the formation that helps us 'understand' the world, when in fact we understand nothing of it. I was involved in a radical part of the feminist movement that caused me to examine everything I did. The whole tradition of art history I was deeply immersed in was male. I was also one of the few women who worked among a group of young male artists. So I initially rejected as much as I could, including the male understanding about art history. I cut up my grid paintings and stitched them together, trying to absorb a tradition that I'd never identified with, which was a woman's tradition of quilting and sewing. I mean, I hated that stuff, but I knew I was going to have to sink myself into it in order to understand the richness there. The movement really gave me permission to be exactly who I was."

Fishman is an artist.

CANDACE BUSHNELL

"Most people associate fashion with style, but I think fashion is just a part of one's style; style is bigger than fashion. Style is the impression you leave people with. Sarah Jessica Parker has something so innate to her style that you can't copy her. Others may copy your fashion, but your style is unique. Though I don't strive for it, it's in my personality to be noticed—not all the time, only when I feel it's necessary. I like things that are glittery and bright! I've worn some pretty outrageous Roberto Cavalli dresses, and I have this Michael Kors dress from the '80s, with long strings of green fringe and a tiny linen shift underneath—it's the ultimate party dress. Even my horse has a bridle made of patent leather and bling. I think it's fun to dress up and put on something a bit outrageous—sometimes if you're close to over the top it makes people feel comfortable, because it's fun. It's about an attitude."

Bushnell is an author.

MARY CERUTI

ON ADMIRATION

"Admiration involves both respect and affection, and mixed in that is this idea of emulation. Worship is different; worship is something that happens at a distance, because when you put someone on a pedestal you're assuming that they have qualities that you're not capable of. But the individuals we admire display qualities that we want to embody. Envy is something I distinguish from admiration, too. Envy shows a lack of independence, a lack of trust in your own convictions. It's ungenerous. It doesn't convey the same respect and affection as admiration. There are certainly circumstances in which one may stop admiring someone else. Especially in this current moment—people you thought were on the right side, and then you find out that they don't have the integrity you thought they did. It comes down to respect."

Ceruti is executive director and chief curator of the Sculpture Center in New York City.

UZODINMA IWEALA

ON ADMIRATION

"In college you're in these creative writing classes where everyone is so angsty and self-important, and you find people writing in the style of writers they admire. That type of imitation is an essential part of development as a creative person. I went through a phase where I was so enamored of Samuel Beckett. I found myself profoundly impacted by the fractured nature of his prose. I thought, Oh, my God, I want to do this. The danger is that you get locked into and frustrated by one particular style. But people grow out of it. It's similar to the way a young person may try to emulate the behaviors of people they admire, like their parents or a sports figure. Eventually your whole worldview will crack the mold of mimicry. You break out, into what is your own self—highly influenced by all the predecessors you've admired but fundamentally your own."

Iweala is an author.

ISABELLA ROSSELLINI
ON ADMIRATION

"My great-aunt Antonietta is one of the first people I remember admiring. She broke the conventions of her day. She was married and had children, but she ran away with her kids to Australia and asked for a divorce—of course, women could not file for divorce in Italy at the time. When the dispute with her husband was settled, she returned and became a race-car driver. There's this photo of her in a race-car hat and big glasses that must have been very controversial. Antonietta was just very simpatico—full of energy, fun, and she loved animals, which I think is something genetic in our family! She shaped for me this idea of 'Why not?' I wouldn't say that I'm courageous, but I have always been guided by this question, 'Why not?' When I went back to university at 60 for my master's degree in animal behavior, I thought of my great-aunt."

Rossellini is an actress, filmmaker and philanthropist.

SIMON DOONAN
ON TASTE

"Good taste is an oppressive concept designed to make people feel ashamed— like they're not quite passing muster. I understand why it was something that people might have talked about in the 1950s, when women wore white gloves, but I can't believe anyone still subscribes to it as something real. I hold to the Quentin Crisp belief that you should not try to keep up with the neighbors—you should drag them down to your level. A lot of this goes back to the Duke and Duchess of Windsor. For some reason, people thought of them as beacons of good taste. Whereas they were really sort of wretched, self-obsessed, vain dandies who were highly entertaining in their own way, but in the end, they were a deranged couple who had nothing to say to each other. They would sit in a restaurant and recite the alphabet. I don't see what's so great about that. I'd rather be Tammy Wynette."

Doonan is an author and the creative ambassador for Barneys.

DIANA
KENNEDY
ON FAILURE

"The simplest dishes are often the most likely to fail, because a simple dish is the test of a good cook: Can you bring out the intrinsic flavors of your ingredients without disguising the other flavors? A good sandwich is also a wicked test. For me there is a difference between really delicious, competent but not so delicious and downright bad. Writers love to take off on me because I am so critical.
For much of my adult life I have been eating superb local food or eating in the restaurants of some of the most distinguished chefs—so at this ripe old age, why shouldn't I have a critical palate? Does anyone, including the chefs who purport to know, stick their necks out and criticize? If I criticize a dish, I am prepared to say why, how it can be improved and, indeed, willing to cook it to prove my point."

Kennedy is a chef, author and expert on Mexican cuisine.

GRETCHEN
RUBIN
ON FAILURE

"Part of failing is figuring out how to fail. There's a real tension, a paradox, in habit formation in that you have to hold two ideas in your head at the same time. On the one hand, failure is no big deal. And on the other hand, you really, really, really don't want to fail, because when you're trying to form a habit, the more you do it the easier it gets. Research shows that sometimes people try to use failure to give themselves more energy—they think if they really load themselves with guilt and shame, it will help them stick to it. But in fact, people who show self-compassion do a much better job of getting back on the horse. There's a great proverb: A stumble may prevent a fall. Instead of saying, This is a catastrophic failure, say, This is the stumble. Now I'm going to learn from it."

Rubin is an author.

VERA
WANG

ON FAILURE

"Very few people who have been in fashion for 45 years are still working. Survival is not a small thing. I feel close to failure every day—I say that very honestly. When you own a company, you worry about your employees. I remember, with every decision I make, that there is a repercussion. And that kind of pressure is hard to live with, especially in a world where everything's public—it takes an enormous toll. You live with that constant sense of possible, imminent failure. But what it all comes back to is the love for the thing itself. In the end, it's not about failure, it's about how much you love what you do. If it gets you up in the morning, gives you a reason to live, a reason to be excited, that's the greatest gift that any passion can give you."

Wang is a fashion designer.

DONALD
KNUTH

ON FAILURE

"In math, we can sort of know that we're wrong. We can even sometimes know that we're right. But with most of science, you could never know that you're right. You can't go to the sun and see what's really there. We make guesses. The main thing is where you set the bar between success and failure. Some people will say 99 percent correct is failure because you made a mistake. With computers, you have to get everything absolutely right. You make one small change to a program, and it crashes. But on a happiness scale, sometimes just 'good' is enough. I think human beings are designed to be 20 percent depressed. Otherwise we wouldn't do anything. We wouldn't have motivation to strive."

Knuth is a computer scientist, mathematician and author.

WILLEM DAFOE
ON COMMITMENT

"Built into commitment is the idea of a promise. The idea itself represents something positive for me, but it also carries with it many associations that are negative: You commit a crime, you're committed to a mental institution, you commit suicide. It can represent a lack of freedom or a surrender. As an actor, you're committing all the time. You give yourself over to these structures and rituals, and you don't always know where they'll take you. The act of giving yourself over to something outside of yourself is valuable because if you serve only yourself, you're limited—limited in imagination and energy. But once you connect and make a commitment to something larger, you begin to take on the energy of that thing. At the heart of pretending, or acting, is a commitment. That quality of engagement is to me the central most important thing in performing."

Dafoe is an actor.

RONI
HORN

"Almost from the beginning, text has found a place in my work. I don't think I ever strongly distinguished language from the visual. Thus titles are important to me both as a reader and an author. Sometimes a title comes along with the work, as part of the invention. *Wonderwater (Alice Offshore)*, which was published as a four-volume set in 2004, uses titles as its starting point and structure. I invited four artists to annotate a selection of my titles. A recent group of drawings is *Remembered Words*. The primary act of the work was literally remembering words. These were then written into the watercolor drawing. And then there are titles with no work associated with them yet. They lie in wait until I understand what they mean. Like *If On a Winter's Night, Then Once Upon a Time*. I'm almost ready to use that one. It's got something to do with fairy tales. Language and visuals occupy the same creative space in my work."

Horn is an artist.

CHESLEY SULLENBERGER

ON TIMING

"Whether it's a crisis or a sudden opportunity, challenges happen on their own schedule. We don't get to decide when we're going to be tested. But you have to be prepared for it, because there isn't time in that moment to learn the things you need to do. I knew landing US Airways Flight 1549 on the Hudson River [on January 15, 2009] was going to be the challenge of a lifetime. I could feel my pulse shoot up, my blood pressure spike, my perceptual field narrow because of the stress. But I had the discipline to compartmentalize and focus. As it turned out, we had just 208 seconds from the time we hit the birds and lost thrust to when we landed in the river. In that time we had to do something we never specifically trained for. So we had to adapt what we did know and apply it in a new way to very quickly solve a problem we'd never seen before."

Sullenberger is an aviation expert and retired airline captain.

MARY KATE CARY

ON TIMING

"In speechwriting, timing means cadence and meter. If you think about music, rhythm can be very calming, and with the spoken word, a deliberate, forceful meter can be motivating. When will.i.am did the Obama speech, he took 'Yes We Can' and turned it into a song, and that's the ultimate example of the musical side of a speech in terms of timing and rhythm. So the first rule before you start writing a speech is to say, What is it that I want people to do? It's not just convincing them about the rightness of your argument— it's motivating them to get off the couch. What speechwriters do is take the prose of a speech and write it on the page as if it were poetry. In George W. Bush's first joint address to Congress after 9/11 he said, 'We will not tire, we will not falter, and we will not fail.' It's like iambic pentameter—it's got that rhythm."

Cary is a political analyst and former White House speechwriter.

MARIA HO

ON LUCK

"It's important for poker players not to get psychologically stuck in the bad luck of a given hand. If you keep lamenting the hand, whether you played it poorly or just got unlucky, then it starts affecting the way you play the next hand and the hand after that. When people get unlucky they start wanting to play badly, and all of a sudden they're in a downward spiral and start to have this if-you-can't-beat-them-join-them mentality. Obviously that route is catastrophic. Poker is a game where your fate is never predetermined. There's a saying in poker: All you need is a chip and a chair. People have come back from tremendous setbacks in the beginning of a tournament and gone on to win it. Poker is not a meritocracy, and sometimes neither is life. Any given player on any given day could beat you. That's the beauty of poker and why it attracts so many players—you can beat the best."

Ho is a professional poker player.

DAVID MILCH

ON LUCK

"My dad was a gambler and a surgeon, and in my endless pursuit of his approval, I gambled too—I sure wasn't going to be a doctor. It distressed him that I seemed to be pissing away my life's possibilities, and I remember he said to me once, 'I don't know how to help you, but if you're lucky, someday you'll meet a man who does know how to help you. And then your proper course in humility will be to follow that luck.' I was lucky enough to meet that man in the author Robert Penn Warren, who was my teacher at Yale. I don't know that I'm capable of defining luck in the abstract, but I know what it means when you have luck—you embrace it and ride it out. The older I get, the less certain I am of what the controlling elements of experience are, and the more consistently I invoke a concept like luck to explain things. It is the unknown expressing itself."

Milch is a writer and producer.

LAURA DERN

ON MANNERS

"It's always thrilling when I meet people, particularly men, whose manners are beautiful. My earliest education in manners came from my Southern grandmother and Southern mother. I was raised to believe that a man opened the door for a lady; he walked down the stairs in front of her so that should she trip and fall he could catch her. A properly raised gentleman considered how he could support a woman, not because she's more delicate, but because it was the right thing to do. So the presidential election has been a true education about manners for me and for my daughter as well. The most offensive quality is the quality of a bully. My grandmother taught me that even when you're angry, you must treat others with respect. You must learn how to rise above."

Dern is an actor.

MAGNUS NILSSON
ON SOLITUDE

"If you aren't used to the wilderness or solitude or open, empty landscapes like we are up here at Fäviken Magasinet restaurant in the middle of Sweden, that can be a very strong, very moving thing for people that travel here from far away. When you travel somewhere for food, the journey becomes part of the whole experience, the whole meal. It's not actually more complicated getting here than anywhere else in Europe, but mentally it feels much more remote. When you live in the countryside, many of the things you do are things you do by yourself. Watercolor painting, fishing, hunting—these are rarely group activities for me. It can be good to be by yourself since there's very little static when you think, but that doesn't necessarily lead to creating dishes. The only real solitude I have in my professional life is the solitude of always being on my own for my decisions, not making them based on someone else's guidelines—the solitude inherent in leadership."

Nilsson is a chef.

TRACEY EMIN

ON SOLITUDE

"I'm very social, but I have to spend a lot of time on my own, because otherwise I can't think properly. I get too much interference from other people's thoughts or feelings or emotions. At the moment I'm in France, surrounded by nature. I might not see anybody for four or five days here. When I first arrive, my nerves are all jangled, but after about three days, I start to think in a very different way. I start to have a dialogue with myself, and that's what I always have to do to make a body of work. I like to wake up early in the winter when it's dark, about 5 o'clock, and the light is coming—that's my favorite part of the day. I think and I write, and there's a silence that's really, really beautiful. What's beautiful about it is you know the day is coming, you know the noise is coming, so it's not forever. It's a magical time—but it's time you have to steal."

Emin is an artist.

RICHARD BRANSON

ON COMPETITIVENESS

"I've been in business since I was 15. In that time, I've seen the importance of competition. We've taken on some of the biggest companies in the world— some for being anticompetitive—and relished the fight. The airline industry is definitely the most competitive. I mean, look at the history of British airlines. British Airways systematically drove out of business anyone who set up in Britain, whether it was British Caledonian, Air Europe or Laker Airways. And they tried to do the same with Virgin Atlantic. Fortunately, when I started the airline, Sir Freddie Laker, the previous person driven out of business, said to me, 'There are only three words that you've got to remember, Richard: *Sue the bastards.* Because they will try the same with you.' And the moment they did, we took them to court and won one of the biggest libel damages cases in history."

Branson, an entrepreneur and philanthropist, is the founder of Virgin Group.

KAMASI WASHINGTON
ON MISTAKES

"I'm from Los Angeles. When I was young, I hung out with gangsters. My mom lived in a Crip neighborhood, and my dad lived in a Blood neighborhood. I used to walk from one neighborhood to the other every day. I had a friend who was a Blood, but he went to a Crip school. He wanted me to walk with him because I knew both Crips and Bloods. He had a gun that he used to keep. We would play *Street Fighter* and then walk to Inglewood. That was a mistake that I used to make daily. I wish I could have slapped myself on the back of my head and said, 'What are you doing?' But it was a mentality. Living in that part of the city didn't affect me. I didn't let it scare me. I was fortunate, though, in that those mistakes didn't end up hitting me too hard. You learn quite a lot from your mistakes, especially those that you make coming from a good place."

Washington is a jazz musician.

BILLY
REID

ON COURAGE

"Courage is more of a mindset than a single act. It's how you approach your life. Courage comes from failure—from the strength of being able to fail. Most people with courage have incredibly positive outlooks. They have a belief that things are going to work out even in the worst of times. It's the old cliché: You can't give up. When I look back at my early career, there were decisions I made to appease a certain retailer, because they thought the collection should be more classic, or whatever. As you mature, you realize it's more important to do the things you want to do. Passion also drives courage—it's part of that mind-set that takes over the fear. Especially when you get to the point where you think 'I believe in myself' and then you watch yourself fail and fail again. You kind of realize what you're made of at those points."

Reid is a fashion designer.

LOIS LOWRY

ON OPTIMISM

"I write for kids, and kids tend to be optimists. Even though I address dark themes in my books, like in *The Giver*, it's always through the eyes of a fictional hero, a young person with integrity, someone a reader can identify with and, in turn, find a kind of integrity and power in themselves. The role of fiction is to rehearse one's life. When kids encounter things in books that they haven't yet faced, they subconsciously rehearse what their reaction will be, how they'll grapple with such things. My mother read *The Yearling* to me when I was a child. Books like that, which affected me profoundly, were about people with realistic problems who forged ahead and overcame them. There's good reason to be pessimistic in this country right now, but I think young people understand that they are the future and hold the power now. It's the power to change the world."

Lowry is an author.

INDEX

COLUMNISTS

Abramovic, Marina, 281
Adelman, Lindsey, 205
Aldrin, Buzz, 67
Anderson, Tracy, 256
Andrés, José, 146
Apfel, Iris, 121
Applebaum, Anne, 178
Amanpour, Christiane, 155
Armisen, Fred, 89
Arnot Reid, Melissa, 187
Atwood, Margaret, 115

Baldessari, John, 35
Barber, Dan, 95
Bass, Anne, 169
Baumeister, Roy, 256
Bernhard, Sandra, 111
Biles, Simone, 15
Blidge, Mary J., 9
Boardman, Samantha, 8
Boone, Mary, 282
Bottura, Massimo, 59
Boulud, Daniel, 167
Bowers, Mary Helen, 158
Boyle, T. C., 265
Branagh, Kenneth, 5
Branson, Richard, 317
Braun, Yael Cohen, 77
Brooks, Danielle, 277
Brosnan, Pierce, 55
Brown, Gavin, 34
Browne, Thom, 250
Buck, Joan Juliet, 94
Burch, Tory, 13
Burns, Christy Turlington, 100

Burns, Ursula, 143
Bushnell, Candace, 297

Campbell, Naomi, 53
Cappellazzo, Amy, 63
Cary, Mary Kate, 309
Ceruti, Mary, 298
Chast, Roz, 51
Cholle, Francis, 268
Chopra, Deepak, 71
Chow, Michael, 227
Chua, Amy, 232
Clementine, Benjamin, 190
Cleveland, Pat, 164
Cohen, Andy, 196
Common, 201
Cousin, Ertharin, 251
Crawford, Cindy, 25
Cucinelli, Brunello, 262
Cumming, Alan, 45

Dafoe, Willem, 305
Daniels, Lee, 159
Danner, Blythe, 227
De Pury, Simon, 182
Dello Russo, Anna, 139
Dern, Laura, 313
Dimitrov, Dimitri, 241
Dixon, Tom, 72
Doonan, Simon, 301
Driver, Minnie, 103
Droga, David, 108
Dufresne, Wylie, 42
Dunbar, Robin, 28
Durant, Kevin, 209

Elbaz, Alber, 189
Elliott, Sam, 197
Emin, Tracey, 315
Englander, Nathan, 161
Erdrich, Louise, 133
Eugenides, Jeffrey, 83

Fellowes, Julian, 279
Fisher, Carrie, 193
Fishman, Louise, 295
Foer, Joshua, 173
Ford, Richard, 229
Franzen, Jonathan, 215
Fraser, Antonia, 239
Fuller, Alexandra, 196

Gabeira, Maya, 289
Gebbia, Joe, 195
Gebre, Mussie, 104
Gervais, Ricky, 185
Gilbert, Elizabeth, 207
Gioni, Massimiliano, 226
Golden, Thelma, 84
Goldin, Nan, 84
Goodall, Jane, 181
Goodwin, Doris Kearns, 81
Gordon, Kim, 208
Gordon-Levitt, Joseph, 105
Grazer, Brian, 27
Grylls, Bear, 79
Guest, Christopher, 269

Haddon, Mark, 104
Hadid, Zaha, 72
Hallberg, David, 132
Hawkins, Paula, 250
Hawn, Goldie, 293

Haynes, Todd, 179
Herman, Susan N., 109
Hetfield, James, 147
Ho, Maria, 310
Hobson, Mellody, 130
Horn, Roni, 307
Howard, Ron, 253
Huffington, Arianna, 7

Isaacs, Cheryl Boone, 276
Ishiguro, Hiroshi, 213
Iweala, Uzodinma, 298

Jenner, Kendall, 41
Judge, Mike, 101
July, Miranda, 289
Junger, Sebastian, 154

Kaling, Mindy, 149
Kalman, Maira, 235
Keflezighi, Meb, 257
Keller, Thomas, 116
Kelley, Kitty, 240
Kendrick, Anna, 186
Kennedy, Diana, 302
Kloss, Karlie, 137
Knuth, Donald, 303
Kondo, Marie, 199
Koons, Jeff, 39
Kors, Michael, 225
Kotb, Hoda, 288
Krakowski, Jane, 145
Kurzweil, Ray, 212

Lagerfeld, Karl, 129
Lebowitz, Fran, 87
Leiber, Judith, 54

Leno, Jay, 165
Lin, Tao, 138
Lithgow, John, 191
Liu, Lucy, 175
Long, William Ivey, 226
Lowry, Lois, 321
Lucci, Susan, 16
Luhrmann, Baz, 61

MacGraw, Ali, 127
Marino, Peter, 73
Maron, Marc, 151
Marshall, Chan, 66
Martin, George R. R., 11
Masson, Charles, 170
Mayne, Thom, 287
McGrath, Pat, 255
McGraw, Dr. Phil, 17
McInerney, Jay, 217
Meester, Leighton, 29
Meiselas, Susan, 91
Menken, Alan, 186
Messud, Claire, 294
Metcalf, Laurie, 178
Meyer, Danny, 80
Milch, David, 311
Miller, Susan, 268
Min, Janice, 283
Miss Piggy, 113
Moretz, Chloë Grace, 288
Muir, David, 276
Murray, Andy, 219
Musto, Michael, 29
Mutu, Wangechi, 179

Nair, Mira, 243
Nars, François, 291

Netrebko, Anna, 233
Nilsson, Magnus, 314
Norwich, William, 221
Notaro, Tig, 197

Oates, Joyce Carol, 223
Olsen, Elizabeth, 231
Ono, Yoko, 249
Osbourne, Ozzy, 247
Ostrovsky, Josh, 251
Ottolenghi, Yotam, 128
Oxman, Neri, 73

Paglia, Camille, 57
Parker, Mary-Louise, 75
Parker, Sarah Jessica, 19
Pasternak, Anne, 285
Patchett, Ann, 23
Patterson, James, 157
Paulson, Sarah, 262
Pawson, John, 158
Perel, Esther, 125
Phillips, Adam, 164
Picasso, Paloma, 117
Pickens, T. Boone, 76

Questlove, 119

Rehm, Diane, 65
Reichl, Ruth, 47
Reid, Billy, 319
Retton, Mary Lou, 142
Ridley, John, 62
Rimoin, Anne W., 259
Ripert, Eric, 203
Ripken, Cal, Jr., 273
Robbins, Apollo, 218

Roble, Stephanie, 80
Roitfeld, Carine, 37
Rossellini, Isabella, 299
Rothblatt, Martine, 263
Rubin, Gretchen, 302
RZA, 112

Saunders, George, 31
Savage, Dan, 135
Schaal, Kristen, 69
Schnabel, Julian, 107
Seacrest, Ryan, 208
Sedaris, Amy, 163
Sedaris, David, 21
Selleck, Tom, 271
Shapiro, Dani, 245
Sharapova, Maria, 116
Simon, Taryn, 141
Simpson, Bart, 48
Simpson, Lorna, 153
Singer, Peter, 183
Smith, Judy, 28
Sorrenti, Mario, 60
Spencer, Octavia, 123
Steber, Maggie, 122
Steel, Danielle, 269
Stewart, Martha, 99
Stine, R. L., 246
Strayed, Cheryl, 3
Stritch, Elaine, 112
Sullenberger, Chesley, 308
Sze, Sarah, 267

Taleb, Nassim Nicholas, 22
Thomas, Kristin Scott, 174
Thurston, Baratunde, 97
Tosi, Christina, 261

Trebek, Alex, 85
Tyson, Neil deGrasse, 43

Versace, Donatella, 93
Von Furstenberg, Diane, 33

Wade, Dwyane, 237
Wambach, Abby, 202
Wang, Vera, 303
Washington, Kamasi, 318
Wasser, Laura A., 90
Waters, Alice, 275
Watts, Reggie, 49
Wearstler, Kelly, 211
Westwater, Angela, 90
Whitesell, Patrick, 62
Wilmore, Larry, 50
Wilson, Rainn, 177
Wojcicki, Anne, 42
Wojcicki, Susan, 272
Wyatt, Lynn, 171

Zimmer, Hans, 131

TOPICS
(with original publication date in *WSJ. MAGAZINE*)

Admiration (March 2018), 273, 298-299
Advice (August 2017), 3, 62-63, 231
Ambition (March 2015), 5, 265, 282-283

Charm (June 2017), 196-197
Color (April 2013), 34-35, 121, 211, 291
Commitment (February 2017), 90-91, 305
Competitiveness (July 2016), 142-143, 317
Confidence (June 2014), 53, 193, 218-219
Courage (March 2015), 123, 289, 319
Curiosity (September 2016), 104-105, 141, 181

Design (May 2013), 72-73
Discipline (March 2013), 8, 128-130, 237, 281

Envy (September 2016), 75, 115, 151, 182-183, 243
Epiphanies (May 2016), 71, 207, 275
Escape (October 2014), 107, 137, 175
Expectations (December 2017), 178-179

Failure (April 2015), 27, 101, 302-303
Fate (October 2015), 250-251
Fear (December 2015), 122, 246-247, 288
Future (November 2014), 42-43, 212

Gossip (May 2017), 28-29

Habit (September 2014), 39, 116-117, 225

Impulse (November 2016), 15, 146-147, 253
Independence (July 2014), 33, 97, 229
Indulgence (December 2013), 9, 93, 217, 279
Innovation (November 2013), 22-23, 149, 261
Intuition (June 2013), 7, 119, 268-269

Language (April 2017), 54-55, 245, 287, 307
Limits (November 2017), 59, 131-133, 174
Love (February 2014), 61, 112-113, 127
Loyalty (March 2016), 65, 201, 262-263
Luck (September 2015), 69, 189, 271, 310-311

Manners (December 2016), 87, 170-171, 313
Memory (September 2014), 84-85, 173, 223
Mistakes (October 2016), 103, 195, 318

Obsession (May 2014), 60, 167, 232-233, 267
Optimism (March 2017), 57, 94-95, 135, 321

Patience (September 2013), 13, 185, 249
Perfection (September 2013), 25, 99, 158-159, 215
Persuasion (September 2017), 37, 108-109, 161
Popularity (February 2018), 157, 205, 272
Possession (June 2016), 164-165
Power (March 2014), 11, 208-209
Procrastination (March 2017), 31, 153, 186-187
Progress (November 2015), 177, 213, 276-277

Risk (July 2013), 79, 154-155, 259

Secrets (March 2016), 16-17, 240-241
Solitude (October 2013), 66-67, 239, 314-315
Status Quo (September 2017), 190-191, 294-295
Strategy (June 2015), 80-81
Style (March 2014), 45, 138-139, 163, 297
Success (December 2014), 76-77, 100

Taste (April 2014), 47, 169, 301
Timing (July 2015), 89, 202-203, 308-309
Transformation (February 2016), 19, 226-227, 255

Vibes (May 2015), 48–49
Vulnerability (October 2017), 83, 125, 285

Willpower (September 2015), 21, 199, 256–257
Wit (April 2016), 50–51, 111, 145, 221

Youth (February 2015), 41, 235, 293

ACKNOWLEDGMENTS

A special shout-out to Chris Ross and Thomas Gebremedhin, who in succession have overseen *WSJ. Magazine*'s Columnists page, and to Chris Knutsen, who collaborated with them and shaped a selection of the interviews into this book. Thanks also to the many people at *The Wall Street Journal* who had a hand in this project, including Ali Bahrampour, Gerry Baker, Magnus Berger, Katie Field, Brekke Fletcher, Adrienne Gaffney, Mike Miller, Sara Morosi, Tanya Moskowitz, Caroline Newton, Clare O'Shea, Sarah Schmidt, Pierre Tardif, Scott White and James Williamson; to our literary representatives at Aevitas Creative Management, particularly David Kuhn and Kate Mack; and to everyone at Black Dog & Leventhal, especially Becky Koh and Frances Soo Ping Chow. Plus a final note of thanks to the artists whose stipple portraits appear in this book: Bill Hallinan, Nancy Januzzi, Hai Knafo, Lura Levy, Bonnie Morrill and Noli Novak.

Black Dog & Leventhal Publishers
Hachette Book Group
1290 Avenue of the Americas
New York, NY 10104
www.hachettebookgroup.com
www.blackdogandleventhal.com

First Edition: September 2018

The interviews in this book originally appeared in *WSJ. Magazine*, which is owned by Dow Jones & Company, Inc.

Black Dog & Leventhal Publishers is an imprint of Running Press, a division of Hachette Book Group. The Black Dog & Leventhal Publishers name and logo are trademarks of Hachette Book Group, Inc.

The publisher is not responsible for websites (or their content) that are not owned by the publisher.

The Hachette Speakers Bureau provides a wide range of authors for speaking events. To find out more, go to www.HachetteSpeakersBureau.com or call (866) 376-6591.

Magnus Berger (Creative Director), Pierre Tardif (Design Director), Katie Field (Designer)

Library of Congress Control Number: 2018937019

ISBNs: 978-0-7624-6563-7 (hardcover); 978-0-7624-6564-4 (ebook)

Printed in the United States of America

LSC-C

10 9 8 7 6 5 4 3 2 1

WSJ. is *The Wall Street Journal*'s award-winning luxury lifestyle magazine; launched as a quarterly in 2008, it is now published 12 times a year. *The Wall Street Journal* is published by Dow Jones, a division of News Corp.

ZZ ALDRIN SOLITUDE CHRISTIANE AMANPOUR RISK
ES IMPULSE MARY J. BLIGE INDULGENCE PIERCE BRO
NDACE BUSHNELL STYLE NERI OXMAN DESIGN DEEPA
JCICKI THE FUTURE WILLEM DAFOE COMMITMENT
DULGENCE YAEL COHEN BRAUN SUCCESS CARRIE FISH
T DIANE VON FURSTENBERG INDEPENDENCE RICKY G
WER BRIAN GRAZER FAILURE BEAR GRYLLS RISK ZAH
N HOWARD IMPULSE ARIANNA HUFFINGTON INTUITI
LOSS ESCAPE MARIE KONDO WILLPOWER PATRICK WI
GERFELD DISCIPLINE FRAN LEBOWITZ MANNERS JAY
ATUS QUO ANN PATCHETT INNOVATION BAZ LUHRMA
OSSIP DR. PHIL MCGRAW SECRETS ANDY MURRAY CON
ARNS GOODWIN STRATEGY AMY CAPPELLAZZO ADVI
TIMISM MARY-LOUISE PARKER ENVY PALOMA PICASS
LIAN SCHNABEL ESCAPE RYAN SEACREST POWER DAV
BES DANIELLE STEEL INTUITION MARTHA STEWART I
ESLEY SULLENBERGER TIMING KRISTIN SCOTT THO
TURE DONATELLA VERSACE INDULGENCE REGGIE WA
ATERS EPIPHANIES LOUISE FISHMAN STATUS QUORAI
LNERABILITY KENNETH BRANAGH AMBITION SAMAN
CHOLAS TALEB INNOVATION ROBIN DUNBAR GOSSIP G
LDESSARI COLOR CARINE ROITFELD PERSUASION TH
MMING STYLE RUTH REICHL TASTE LARRY WILMORE
ASSIMO BOTTURA LIMITS MARIO SORRENTI OBSESSIC
ANE REHM LOYALTY CHAN MARSHALL SOLITUDE KRI
ANG FAILURE T. BOONE PICKENS SUCCESS STEPHANIE
LDIN MEMORY MARIA HO LUCK RICHARD BRANSON